OPTIC

GAMING

DEY ST.
AN IMPRINT OF WILLIAM MORROW *PUBLISHERS*

OPTIC GAMING

The Making of eSports Champions

H3CZ   BigTymeR

NaDeSHoT   Scump

OpTicJ   MiDNiTE

Fwiz

HarperCollins books may be purchased for educational, business, or sales promotional use. For information please e-mail the Special Markets Department at SPsales@harpercollins.com.

FIRST EDITION

Designed by Suet Yee Chong

Library of Congress Cataloging-in-Publication Data has been applied for.

ISBN 978-0-06-244928-3

16 17 18 19 20   OV/RRD   10 9 8 7 6 5 4 3 2 1

We dedicate this book to every member of OpTic,
Past, Present, and Future, and every member of the Green Wall.

CONTENTS

PART 1

THE BIRTH
OF OPTIC

A VERY HUMBLE BEGINNING

OpTicJ

I have no idea where the name OpTic came from. Chalk that up as the number one mystery to this day. The best guess we've been able to come up with is that the name has something to do with optics or visuals—like an optic lens in the scope of a sniper rifle. In the beginning, OpTic was a sniping team and we became very popular for using the sniper rifle in the game, so that seemed like a natural fit. I could be wrong. Who knows?

The first time I ever heard of *Call of Duty* was back when I was in college at Arizona State. This was early 2004. I saw my buddy playing *Call of Duty 1* on a PC in his dorm room and he was just raving about how awesome it was, but I didn't pick it up right away. The game didn't completely register with me until a year later when I bought my first Xbox 360 and started playing *Call of Duty 2*. I played the campaign and jumped into multiplayer. Scoping in and being able to kill people with one shot on a sniper rifle was just fascinating to me. It looked so realistic.

The game has come a long way since then. For those of you

who can remember, *Call of Duty 2* was so incredibly different because there weren't any perks. There weren't any of the power-ups like there are in today's games that could juice you as a player and make you better. It literally came down to my shot being better than my opponent's. If it wasn't, then I was going to get killed. It was that simple. The game was about raw gun skill and that's what got me hooked on the series.

Not only was the game evolving, but video games in general were completely changing. When Xbox Live came out at the end of 2005, people were now able to sit in their living rooms and play online with people from all over the country. My introduction to online gaming was the *Tom Clancy's Rainbow Six: Rogue Spear* series, but competitive *Call of Duty* was beginning to gain a following. I found a group of people online who shared this same interest and a community was formed. We were always talking about which gun to use, how to use it, and what other players we should be watching. I had joined a couple different clans (they're just called teams now, but at the time everyone called them clans) and we would play competitive matches against other clans. The community was so small back then that everybody knew each other.

I was in a clan called Cereal Killers. That's not a typo—we spelled it like breakfast cereal. Our idea was to be this goofy-named team who went around destroying people and that's exactly what we did. We were really good at it, and I quickly developed a reputation for being one of the better snipers. The problem was that we couldn't keep the team together. Some people would secretly join another team, some people would get booted, and others would leave simply because they thought someone was lying. Once those relationships within the team were strained, chemistry suffered and we started to lose. Sure enough, Cereal Killers fell apart. I still wanted to play, but the drama was taking its toll. I wanted to get back to the root of it all and play with my pals for fun. So when it came to finding a new clan, I took a different approach.

One of the clans that I grew to respect was called Dog Company.

What drew me to them was that they were known for using a sniper rifle. It was about precision and skill with them, which is where I felt my talent lay at the time, so they would be a good fit. They were very small and humble. Their leader was this guy named Casey Bartow, who had just recently changed the name of the clan from Dog Company to OpTic. I wanted to join, but I didn't want to tell them who I was. I didn't want to be affiliated with my old clan at all. I wanted a fresh start.

I decided to ditch my old Cereal Killer gamer tag and randomly generated a new one so I could pose as an unknown. I managed to track down Casey, who I knew only as OpTic KR3W then, and one of his teammates when they were playing on a map called Vossenack. It's a very small map, usually used when players wanted to settle a 1v1 sniper challenge. Once I saw them in there, I pulled out a sniper rifle and just started tearing them apart. That got their attention, so I asked Casey if they were holding tryouts. It was kind of a joke at first, but he was cool about it. He said, "If you beat us, you can join." So I started beating them, and as promised, they invited me to join the team. After that, I finally told them who I really was.

GAMER TAG TALES

Since we spelled Cereal Killers like the breakfast cereal, we all named ourselves after popular cereals. I was Pops . . . CK Pops. I ditched that when I tried out for OpTic and the random gamer tag I generated was Willy Jones. It sounded dumb enough, so I went with it. When I joined OpTic, it became OpTic Jones even though I have no affinity with the name Jones. I don't even have a *J* in my name. As time progressed I changed it to OpTicJ. And today, I'm the only member of OpTic who doesn't have a space separating OpTic from his name.

There were about twelve members in OpTic at the time, and soon after I joined, they wanted to find a new leader. KR3W was very young. He was finishing high school and getting ready to go to college. Sometimes people would see him as an oddball and he didn't always get along with everyone else. There were older and more mature players on the team better suited for that leadership role. I think KR3W was unfairly looked at as this sore thumb who was just in the way, so he was uprooted.

In the end, we wanted to get along and we wanted to win. In order to play at the highest level possible we needed someone with more real-world experience to lead that charge. That's when I stepped up to become a coleader, which back then didn't mean much. It was more of a vanity title. There was no money involved. We weren't even recording ourselves playing. YouTube hadn't been created, so people weren't uploading content.

What most people don't realize is that OpTic wasn't very well liked or respected in the beginning. We were kind of thought of as being these cheese-ball amateurs. We had a good reputation on a site called NxGamers, but that website was looked at as second tier. If you were a serious player and wanted to compete against the best clans at the highest level in eSports at that time, you had to play on GameBattles. The problem was that we were sponsored by NxGamers, so we had to play exclusively on their site. Both sites were competing against each other to get more traffic and sponsoring teams was their way to attract more players. We were stuck for the time being.

The bigger problem with playing online was that it was difficult to document these games since nobody was recording footage or using capture cards. We relied on screen shots, but if you forgot to take a screen shot and somebody reported a different score, you were screwed. We could report that we beat a certain team, but they could just as easily say that they won. The cheating and the lying became so rampant that the owners of the website said that if we were going to play a match then we had to get a referee. That referee would be a neutral official who would verify the result.

Hector Rodriguez was a referee who was just getting into *Call of Duty* and was always available online. He was an all-around good guy and a fan of OpTic, so we wanted him to ref our matches. He was also an adult and not a kid trying to get attention. He was humble in his approach and not that guy who was constantly knocking on the door asking to join the team. His reputation was strong as a community advocate, and to us that was extremely valuable because we were this homegrown, family-oriented team. We were a group of friends who were trying to win competitive matches and have fun while hanging out playing video games. Hector fit the profile perfectly, so we talked about inviting him to join OpTic.

We were a little apprehensive at first. The problem was that if Hector joined OpTic, then he couldn't ref our matches because it would be a conflict of interest. We already weren't well liked in the community, so this could further tarnish our reputation. We went back and forth, but in the summer of 2006 we ended up pulling the trigger and bringing Hector on board. It proved to be a smooth transition. We weren't playing that many matches on NxGamers, and since it was difficult to get a match every day, we reached a point where we had to make the transition to GameBattles.

Here we were, all set to take a giant leap forward and play better competition, when suddenly the scene just died. *Call of Duty 3* proved to be a terrible sequel, so most of us in the community went back to playing *Call of Duty 2*. Very little happened until *Call of Duty 4* came out in 2007. That game was just really tight. It was easy to move around, and when it came to hit markers, people would die when they were supposed to die. Not all the time, but it was pretty darn accurate. It had all these new fascinating guns that were really fun to use.

But the most important addition was a perk system. You could now assign abilities and attributes to help the way your character played the game. You might be able to take more damage, or pick up extra grenades. The game also had kill streaks that would reward you for being a good player, so the rich get richer. If you got a three-kill streak, you'd have the ability to call up UAV and see other players on the map. However, because of the perk system, other players could hide from that UAV. If you got five kills, you would get this air strike. If you got seven, this helicopter would come down. All of this really started to revolutionize the way we played video games. Players now had the ability to become a weapon themselves—not like the previous games, which were strictly about gun skill. It was super addicting and the game caught on quick.

Playing online was fun, but the idea of going to an actual event to play against other teams live and in person sounded awesome. In November 2007, OpTic participated in our first-ever eSports LAN (local area network) tournament in Orlando, Florida. It was being held at the Hard Knocks, which was a LAN center for video games and laser tag. This was a 3v3 tournament sponsored by NxGamers and the winner would get $2,000. Hector and I teamed up with OpTic Carlton, and we all paid our own way to fly down to Orlando and play.

We had no idea how we were going to do, but nobody cared. Everyone in this online community at the time liked each other. We were going there to compete, but for us it was more about the opportunity to meet in person. We wanted to hang out, have a good time, and see where this could take us. If you were playing video games at this time, the people you were playing with were people you met online. It wasn't until a few years later that there were more opportunities to meet some of these people at gaming events. KR3W is the guy who recruited me into OpTic and I've known him for nine years, but I've still never met him in person.

Orlando was really fun, but this wasn't a well-organized tournament. There were about ten teams total. The brackets were determined on the spot. One of the tournament organizers was in the corner writing everything out on a whiteboard. There were no commentators or broadcasters. It wasn't live-streamed. Updates on who won and who did what were posted in a forum. This wasn't a high-end production; it was very user-generated content. In the end, we did okay and finished third, but there was no cash take-home prize for third. Since we had to pay our own way, we essentially lost money and paid to play, but it was a blast.

As the year went on I found myself playing less and less with OpTic. I had just graduated college and I wound up taking the first job I interviewed for—an HR position at the Arizona State Credit Union. In addition to a full-time job I also had a new girlfriend who I worked with. Real life began to set in, so I couldn't keep in touch with the community like I used to. I could only play during the week, so my involvement was more low-key.

As soon as I took over the team from KR3W, Hector was the go-to guy for me when we were doing anything. It was nice to have him around. As an older guy, he was levelheaded and had a career. He made smart decisions and understood the gaming community. So when I made the decision to step down in 2007, he was undoubtedly the right person for the job. Looking back, I think he did pretty good work. =)

2

AN ESCAPE AFTER WORK

H3CZ

The first thing that people notice about Ryan is his high-pitched voice. It's hard to describe. You really have to hear it, but people just get attached to it, or sometimes even annoyed by it. Go check out one of his live streams and you'll know exactly what I mean. For the first year I was in OpTic, I identified Ryan by his voice because I had only seen this one blurry picture of him online.

It wasn't until I was in that Orlando hotel lobby in 2007 that I came face-to-face with this guy who would later become one of my best friends. I had paid $656 for hotel and airfare to play in the LAN tournament. I got there first and was checking in at the front desk when I could hear that very distinct voice on the other side of the wall. It was hard to comprehend that I was about to finally meet the actual guy that I've been talking to for the past year. I almost didn't even go to this tournament because a part of me thought it was ridiculous that I was about to pay all this money to fly out to Florida so I could play a video game. It was my girlfriend, Judith, who convinced me. "You hang out with them all the time. Go meet them."

I didn't play a lot of video games growing up. The first thirteen years of my life were spent in Juarez, Mexico, before my parents moved our family to the Chicago suburb of Wheeling. I was a graffiti artist and I loved to fish. With the exception of poker, most everything I did was outside. So when Judith and I were furniture shopping for our first apartment in 2004, she was baffled when I suddenly wanted to buy this Xbox. I hadn't owned a system since my Nintendo 64 in high school. "That's just gonna sit there and collect dust," she told me. And it wasn't like I had all the free time in the world. I had a good job working in the mortgage industry and was doing really well for a twenty-four-year-old kid, but for whatever reason something compelled me to buy an Xbox that day. If she'd asked me "why?" one more time, she might have easily talked me out of it.

Call of Duty was the game that came with the Xbox. As soon as I started playing I was blown away and I quickly beat the game on campaign mode. Everything in the game was so real-looking. I was always into war movies—sniper movies in particular. *Sniper, Enemy at the Gates*—anything that involved a strategic approach to winning a war sucked me in.

I wanted to learn more about the game and I kept reading about being able to play online. I didn't know what that meant, but I gave it a shot. Xbox came with a free three-month trial. I didn't have a headset or anything, but signed on and found my way onto this map where people were playing. I kept hearing this chatter and had no idea what was going on. At first I thought the voices were part of the game, but these people sounded like kids. "H3CZ, come over here!" As soon as they started calling me by my gamer tag, I realized that these were other people online.

"I'm not going over there. You're gonna kill me," I told him.

"No, I'm not," he said. "We're on the same team."

Oh my God. This is a thing. That sense of connection that I had with a complete stranger got me hooked. I immediately went out and bought a headset so I could start communicating. It felt like playing pickup basketball the way teammates would congratulate me after the game. The game itself wasn't addicting; it was how good I was at it that left me wanting to play more. From there I started to learn about competition and strategy. I obviously wanted to win, but I also wanted to be better than my teammates. I wanted to enter a lobby and have others recognize me as a professional.

GAMER TAG TALES

I was fourteen years old and had been in the United States for a year when I became interested in the art of graffiti. I needed a nickname. My name was Hector Rodriguez, so I took the first three letters of my first name and the last letter of my last name. I didn't want to be Hex because that was already taken, so I took HECZ. When I started drawing it I saw the symmetry between the 3 and the Z, so it stuck with me through junior high and into high school. Now it's my name.

As I grew more interested in competitive gaming so did my brother, Pedro, who was ten years younger than me. I kept telling him, "There are a ton of teams out there. Why can't we make our own?" I thought if somebody else can do it, why can't I? I didn't want to just start a team; I wanted to start the best team. That's always been my mentality no matter what I was doing. That's how PlagueX was born.

The game became an escape after long days at work. When I was a kid, all I wanted to do was have a job where I wore a suit and tie to work. To me that represented money and success. That's what I had, but it didn't seem like success now, and when the mortgage industry crashed, it was a rude awakening that I wasn't prepared for. I went to work for AIG at a significant pay cut and had to change the way I was living. The only thing that allowed me to disconnect from that harsh reality was being good at a video game.

One time I was playing in a public match and I saw this guy named OpTic Preview come into the game. He beat everyone in a way that I'd never seen before. At first I thought he was using in-game cheats, but I started to watch him closely. I stayed out of the next game just to see what he was doing and realized that there was no way he could be cheating. He was missing and making mistakes, but still winning decisively. The next day, I started playing and saw somebody else with the name OpTic and realized that OpTic was a team. I thought he was going to be really good, but I ended up beating this guy. *If I beat him, why couldn't I be a part of this team?* So I started stalking his account. Every time he'd join a lobby, I'd join, and I just kept beating him over and over again.

I looked up OpTic and learned that they competed on a website called NxGamers, so that's where I went next. On every tournament website there is a volunteer section. I put my name down on a list of people who wanted to be referees and waited to be contacted. When I was selected, my job was to watch the matches between teams and then report the score. Selfishly, I wanted to learn from the pros. Watching how professional players maneuvered around the map was priority number one, so I gladly volunteered my time to do it for free. I wanted to study the game and learn their strategies. Nobody would allow me to do this on my own, but once I became an official, they would have no choice but to let me spectate.

Ryan Musselman was already on OpTic. He was really good at the game. The first time OpTic needed a ref, I struck up a conversation with him. He was a little bit older than the rest of the guys on the team, so we had that connection. He was going to college and had a job, so he had real-life experience. Oftentimes it would just be me and Ryan waiting in the lobby for the rest of the players. Slowly, we developed a friendship and started hanging out every single day online as I reffed their matches. When OpTic wasn't playing, I'd come in to crack jokes and have fun with them. Eventually, he invited me onto the team.

I was having dinner with my family when I told my brother that I had been invited to join OpTic. "Holy shit! You gotta join," he told me. "But what about Plague?" I asked. "Don't worry. OpTic is a better team and this is a better opportunity. Just join."

So that's what I did.

H3CZ RANKS
THE *CALL OF DUTY* TITLES

My favorite *Call of Duty* by far is *Call of Duty 4*. In those days it was all about reputation, so we were all a little more passionate. It was a daily grind. I couldn't wait to get home from work and hop on for hours on end. I would play late into the night even though I knew that I would have to wake up early for work. I'm going to put *Ghosts* on this list as well, because we grinded that game just like we did years earlier in *Call of Duty 4*. We were playing every night and streaming. This got us a crazy amount of viewership—not because of our skill, but because of our banter.

1. *Call of Duty 4*
2. *Call of Duty 2*
3. *Black Ops 2*
4. *Ghosts*

Little by little, Ryan let go of the team. Later that year, he got a girlfriend and said, "I quit video games. I'm gonna go live life and have fun. This is now your team. Do with it what you want." At this point there was no money involved. There were no sponsors or legalities whatsoever. When Ryan left, I could have easily started my own team and named it something else, but I kept my name as OpTic H3CZ and kept the team as OpTic Gaming.

The first thing I did was recruit my brother, Pedro, onto the team and he became OpTic Tumors. Right away he made a very significant contribution. He came up to me and said, "Hey, man, there's this guy on YouTube making videos. I know I'm better than him. Can you buy me a capture card so I can make my own videos?"

I knew nothing about capture cards or YouTube, so my brother told me how you could now record yourself playing the game and post it online. He showed me this guy named zzirGrizz who created this montage video where he got over a hundred comments on You-Tube. Nobody else was doing this at the time. Immediately I wanted to do what this guy was doing. I bought my brother a capture card and we started making videos. This was when I decided to turn OpTic into a video-game entertainment platform. We were going to do tutorials and showcase the best of the best. We wanted to be the best team around and we were going to provide video proof. The passion came from two places. It came from earning a reputation for being the best at something. It also came from seeing our videos gaining in popularity.

At the beginning of 2009, I was still working at AIG, but all I thought about at work was OpTic and where I wanted to take the company. My productivity was going down. It was a grind. Every day I'd wake up at the same time. On the drive to work I'd see the same cars on the road. It felt like I was stuck in that office waiting for something bigger to happen. The Rolodex calendar where I kept my schedule was filled with ideas about where I wanted to take OpTic. I'd come home from work every day and make videos, create content, and hope that somebody would watch it. Sometimes I'd even skip work to play all day. I stopped talking to friends and barely talked to Judith anymore on the weekends. Something was telling me that I was supposed to be working in video-game entertainment. The vision I had of myself wearing a suit and tie to work every day was not what I wanted anymore.

So when AIG was making job cuts after the government bailout, I walked into my manager's office and we mutually agreed to part ways. I figured that if I wasn't making much money, I might as well try doing something I love. Judith was seven months pregnant at the time, so it was crazy that she went along with this idea, but she let me do it. My manager told me, "Hey, look on the bright side. Every-thing happens for a reason." At first that rubbed me the wrong way. She knew that I wasn't getting paid much and my first kid was on the way, but it turned out she was right. Everything did happen for a reason. As scary and as uncertain as that moment was, it was also my proudest moment. At twenty-nine years old, I jumped in headfirst and cut myself off from that safety net previously provided by corporate America.

Now it was all about OpTic and once again it was my brother who inspired the next big move. He played because he was having fun and he was really good at it. Specifically, he was a really good sniper. He didn't use regular weapons. He only used a bolt-action sniper rifle, so I decided to give it a try and played public matches with only the sniper rifle. The more I used it the better I got and the more I felt a sense of accomplishment because using only a sniper rifle puts you at a disadvantage. You can only fire one bullet every three seconds against people who were shooting fifteen bullets at you every second.

Based off this one concept, we decided to create a sniper team and this was something people responded to right away. We were the first-ever legitimate sniper clan. Nobody on the team was allowed to use another weapon. We wanted to show how good we were using the hardest weapon in the game. The competitive side of me came out again. I told the team, "We're gonna play against everybody out there. You can't say no if you're challenged to a match. If you lose, you're off the team." From us, every other sniper clan was spawned. We recruited two of the absolute best snipers in the community in Preda-tor and DTreats. This was also when Hutch came on board before he went on to become one of the first big personalities in *Call of Duty*.

Hutch was the first person to land a contract with Machinima, a multichannel network that was one of the first big movers in the gaming scene on YouTube. This meant that he could make money off of his YouTube videos. It turns out he was only getting what amounted to something like two dollars for every thousand views,

H3CZ'S TOP OPTIC SNIPERS

This was a really difficult list to compile because we had so many good snipers, but if I was forced to rank them in order (not including myself, of course), this is how I'd do it. What set these guys apart was their passion for the specific weapon. It's funny because unless you're a sniper for *Call of Duty,* you'll never understand it. You're either a sniper or you're not. Even after not using the sniper rifle for two years, I still consider myself a sniper.

1. DTreats
2. Predator
3. Pamaj
4. Hutch

but I didn't care about that. The second I heard that I could make money off videos, my world opened up. If we could make $5 off of a video, why couldn't we turn that into $500? And if we could make $500 off a video, why couldn't we make $500,000? And if we were making that much money, why couldn't we just make millions? That was my vision. I was going to focus entirely on this. It was going to be my life's work, and OpTic was going to be a team that people wanted to be associated with.

Now we had to make our mark. The day before *Modern Warfare 2* was released in November 2009, I planned to post a montage for the game because I knew it would get a lot of views. With this video, I wanted to capture as big of an audience as possible so we could become the next big thing. I went out and bought an illegal Xbox. I bought a pirated game. I had literally four hours to play it and get cold footage. I then had to give all of that footage to the editor, who had one day to cut it together before we uploaded the video. Not only did this video explode, but it put us over the edge and told everyone that OpTic was THE *Call of Duty* team. We were the ones to watch. We were doing something new. Off that video, and with help from Hutch, I was able to get a partnership with Machinima. Now we were legitimate and this led to hypergrowth right across the board. That video is still up today and has over six million views.

Everything started to fall into place. I created a series called *Top Five Kill Cam* on Machinima that was starting to take off. We started a main hub channel called OpTic Nation and were also able to give ten members of OpTic their own channels on Machinima. In addition to creating personalized content for their own channels, all the members of OpTic could now contribute to the same channel. This allowed the fans to get to know everybody.

3

PLAYING VIDEO GAMES
FOR A LIVING

OpTicJ

nytime I tell somebody not in the industry that I work in gaming, they assume that I'm a game tester or something. That's what my parents thought I did when I got my first job, and I'm pretty sure that's what they still think I do.

When I was a kid, being a game tester would have been my dream job. Little did I know that it wasn't one of the more prestigious jobs in the industry. I loved gaming ever since I was a little kid growing up in Gilbert, Arizona. The first time I saw anything video-game related was when I was five and watched my friend's parents playing *Pitfall* back in the eighties. They had to jump on the heads of alligators to get across a pond and swing on ropes. Immediately I loved it and wanted to play so bad, but nobody would let me. This happened again a few years later when *Mario Bros.* came out on Nintendo. It was like a carrot being dangled in my face, but a carrot with a whole bunch of candy and presents on it. When I finally did get to play, it was the most exciting thing ever. I was actually controlling the visuals on the screen. A passion was already developing and I was instantly hooked.

I always wanted to work in gaming, but I had absolutely no clue how to go about doing that. The path that led me to where I am today was inevitable even though I totally didn't see it at the time. Once I finished college, I was trying to figure out what I wanted to do for a career. While at Arizona State, I bounced around between majors. I started in criminal justice and then went to advertising and marketing before finally ending up with a communications degree. I assumed that I would enjoy working in human resources because I wanted to be a recruiter. Recruiting, managing, and evaluating people were all things that I was good at. It took about six months before I realized that I absolutely hated that job. Maybe some people enjoy working in HR, but I was not one of those people. I was building up a little resentment as well because this was the job that took me away from gaming to begin with. I needed to get out, but I didn't know what to do next.

In March of 2010, I reconnected with a couple of old friends I had played with during *Call of Duty 2*. These were guys I knew even before OpTic. We put aside old grievances and decided to get back together to play in this one online tournament Machinima was putting on. The first-place team would get a cash prize and the second-place team would get a capture card to make videos and a Machinima contract to upload those videos to the Internet. Looking at it now, this was kind of backward because the second prize was way better than the first prize since the capture card would allow you to make more money by uploading videos. We ended up taking second place and winning the Machinima contract.

I had no idea what this meant, so I called up Hector and started telling him about the tournament and the capture card. He stopped me and said, "Let me tell you something. There is money to be made. You need to get involved in this." H3CZ started teaching me about the business, and how they were making money from advertisements on YouTube. They were getting paid something like two dollars for every thousand views they got. It didn't sound all that good, but he was like, "No, it's good because my videos are getting millions of views." At that moment he had me hook, line, and sinker. For the first time ever, someone could potentially make a living by playing video games.

Hector was about to take the company in a radical new direction. OpTic was always known as a sniper clan, but Hector was going to the next level. He took a very popular component of the game and exploited it. All the while, *Call of Duty* was becoming one of the most popular games of its time; arguably the most popular. Hector always thought it would be amazing if people could do this for a living, and it was the creation of capture cards that allowed us to eventually do that by recording game-play footage. Once you could put ads on that recorded footage, you've basically reinvented television for the Internet.

OPTICJ RANKS THE CALL OF DUTY TITLES

Call of Duty 2 will always be my favorite game. That game to me was the forging of a multiplayer experience online. I also have sentimental reasons because it was through this game that I got to meet all the people in real life who I had only met online. I met really good friends like H3CZ. Nine years later, he would be one of the groomsmen in my wedding, and it was all because of this game. *Black Ops 2* is definitely a better game than *Black Ops 1,* but I just didn't play that game as much, so I put *Black Ops 1* ahead of it. All the games on my list are on it because of the specific multiplayer experiences I had, which is what always drew me to the series and video games in general.

1. *Call of Duty 2*
2. *Modern Warfare 2*
3. *Call of Duty 4*
4. *Black Ops 1*
5. *Black Ops 2*

In March 2010, I decided to make my triumphant return to OpTic. This was when I started my Twitter account and created my YouTube channel. I uploaded a few videos to Machinima Respawn. I was mostly making *Call of Duty* and *Battlefield* videos. The first video I ever posted was a montage of my favorite shots from *Battlefield* set to an Eminem soundtrack. This was before content ID set in, so we could use popular mainstream songs. I was getting used to the whole process of recording game-play footage and talking over it. In those days, live commentaries weren't common. People would usually record the game play and then add voice-over after about the game or even random topics like how to get a girl. Everyone's style and approach was different. It was all about figuring out what steps to take to create your own unique voice.

I wanted to focus on being our community director. That meant talking to fans directly and creating a place for them to view our content. That's why I created my channel. I thought of it as an OpTic community channel. This was early 2010 and OpTic was gaining popularity on YouTube. Everyone wanted to be a part of OpTic—and to this day we still get a ton of questions about how to join. So I came up with this idea to launch a competition. It would be an *American Idol*–style show where the winner got a chance to join. We would record videos, hold tryouts, and heavily promote it. I did this all on my channel and one of the requirements was that you had to subscribe.

I'd basically hold this open lobby where anyone could join. So fifteen or twenty people would square off in this sniper competition to see who would become the next OpTic sniper. You could only use certain rifles, scopes, and perks. As they were playing, I'd watch to see who had the best technique. I'd look for the little things, like who could land shots consistently and pull up the scope fastest. This went on for a couple weeks and we ultimately found a new player in OpTic Rated. It was fun, and this was one of the ways that I began to grow my audience and get those new subscribers to view my content. It helped my channel blow up real fast and in the process I could relaunch my own identity within OpTic, which I had lost when I was gone.

OPTICJ: PLAYING VIDEO GAMES FOR A LIVING   //   25

Another series I created was called *Tar Play*. There was a gun in *Modern Warfare 2* called the Tar. It was a little sporadic in the way it shot, but it was super powerful and fun to use. I could get some really cool game play with it. I knew that people liked montages, but they also liked commentary, so what I decided to do was go play with this gun all the time and get some good clips. Instead of doing a montage, I put all of the clips into one video. I then invited friends like H3CZ and Di3seL to do this three-way commentary. It was more like a podcast over these really cool game-play clips.

I loved making videos. I was having fun with my pals and making a little money on the side, but in the back of my head I still wanted to work in the industry. We had a good relationship with Machinima, so I asked if they had any job openings. I heard about how people who work there were able to produce content and that's what I wanted to do. I knew I had a lot to learn, but I felt equipped to be a good businessman in the industry. I grew up in gaming, but I wasn't totally hip to what was happening on YouTube. I wasn't a YouTuber, and I didn't watch a lot of YouTube videos, but I knew enough to get started. If I could begin to build those relationships I could become a valuable asset one way or another. It didn't hurt to ask, but Machinima gave me the runaround and told me they'd keep me posted. Meanwhile, I kept making videos.

One of the early problems we had with Machinima was that it took a superlong time to actually get paid. They had a lot of directors, so once you submitted a video, it would take a couple of weeks before that video actually went up on the site. It would then take about six months before we saw any money. You couldn't run a business like that unless you made an absolute killing and could survive until the next six-month pay period. So when Machinima's rival Maker Studios approached OpTic with a deal saying we could get paid monthly, and also get paid on our individual channels, we jumped at the chance and signed a contract. Now we didn't have to wait to get paid and they even offered us a higher revenue share.

We broke the news to Machinima that we were leaving for Maker

Studios and Machinima got super upset. They threatened to take down our videos if we left, and in an attempt to keep us, they offered us the same deal Maker did so we could get paid on our individual channels. We never really wanted to leave, so we agreed. They even talked to the Maker executives to get us out of the deal we just signed with Maker. Looking back at this now, we were so green at the time and had no idea what we were doing. We were fortunate that things worked out the way they did.

Machinima was more popular in the gaming scene than Maker. They were also a better fit for our company and what we wanted to do because they were hyperfocused on gaming. Maker was more of a vlog and entertainment station that was into comedy and music. Machinima was hard-core gaming. It was the center of gaming and *Call of Duty* on the Internet, which was appetizing for me because I didn't care that much about comedy or music. I grew up with gaming, and if we were going to post our videos to a channel, I wanted it to be a channel that specialized in gaming.

OpTic was back at Machinima and had a better deal, which was great, but I was still working in human resources and miserable. For a while Machinima gave me the runaround when it came to landing a full-time job. After some back-and-forth between Machinima, OpTic, and me, during which it looked like I might take a job working full-time for Maker, I landed a job at Machinima and negotiated a better deal for OpTic so we could profit from our videos and also get paid on our individual channels. It was a HUGE win for OpTic.

The cherry on top was that I found a way to work in gaming and make a living without having to be a programmer or a professional player who had to rely on a couple hundred dollars in tournament winnings here and there. I could now create content for a living at Machinima. By August 2010, this was now my full-time job and that was amazing.

4

BORN AND RAISED IN ESPORTS

Fwiz

Part of me felt that all this attention OpTic got back then was bullshit.

When I first heard of OpTic, I had been on the eSports side of *Call of Duty* while working at Major League Gaming and commentating live matches on the side. I was always a part of competitive gaming even though it was still very much in its infancy. In the eSports community, there was a lot of animosity toward people like Hector and Hutch for making sniper videos on *Call of Duty*. I admit that they were fun to watch. Don't get me wrong, those guys were entertainers, but they sure as hell weren't pro players. People loved the sniper videos and OpTic was very good at it, but they were getting more attention and notoriety for making videos and being on YouTube than eSports players were getting for playing the actual game. That didn't sit right with me. I always thought the competitive players who were highly skilled and talented should be the ones getting the attention. Now I realize how wrong I was. This was just me being naive at the time because, even today, entertainment in gaming is just as big as eSports.

I always loved video games. The only thing I loved more than video games was being good at videos games. I started playing when I was three after my mom bought a Nintendo for my older brother, and I haven't stopped playing since. By the time I was fourteen and in high school, I was playing a ton of competitive *Counter-Strike*. I loved being able to play online and I met so many other people just like me all over the country.

All the while I was playing regular sports too. I loved baseball, and I played lacrosse until I got to high school. So when I stumbled upon eSports as a fourteen-year-old kid, it made all the sense in the world to me. Here was my love of sports and video games literally being tied together. The competition, the camaraderie with teammates, and the dynamic of being a leader were now all being positioned digitally within a video game.

As I got older, I found myself focusing much more on my video-game skill set than trying to pursue baseball in any serious manner. I was just more interested and passionate about video games. I had ADHD, so maybe video games did a better job of keeping my attention. I have no idea. I was always baffled by how you couldn't get me to sit still at a table for five minutes, but I could stare at my computer for eight hours and play video games without moving. It's something my mom and I still talk about. She used to tell me, "There's no way you have ADHD because you sit in front of that damn thing for hours at a time."

By the time I got to Ohio State, I had to figure out a way to do this for a living. I was incredibly adamant about that, but I wasn't sure how to do it because there were so many different ways to go about working in the gaming industry. Should I pursue marketing for games? Should I be a game designer? Should I get involved with sales? One particular area didn't stand out or appeal to me more than another. All the while I kept playing.

In 2007, I came across a website called GameBattles. I wanted to keep playing competitively, but the guys I used to play *Counter-Strike* with were no longer around. At that time, *Counter-Strike* was on a

GAMER TAG TALES

It's not that exciting of a story at all. I've been called Fwiz for something like seventeen years now. I'll be honest, I don't even know if this story is true, but I've said it so many times that I'm starting to believe that it is. I generated my gamer tag on Xbox. Four-letter gamer tags were really rare to have on Xbox, and I just wanted one so it would look unique. I found one in Fwiz, but I don't know what it means or how I came up with those four letters. It might have been the sound of it, or just some joke I had at the time with my friends. I've been asked this so many times, so I should probably do my due diligence to get to the bottom of it. In all fairness, I came up with this name so long ago while I was messing around on Xbox Live. Who was I to think that one day this would become the name people know me by. Shit, man, I was just trying to play *Halo*. Fwiz? Sure.

major decline. It didn't have that support from an eSports perspective until the title experienced a resurgence years later in 2014. Over that summer, I found a couple buddies online (God knows where those guys are today) and we started playing *Call of Duty 2* together, but it was when *Call of Duty 4* came out the following November that everyone went bonkers.

I wasn't playing competitive *Call of Duty* long before I realized that I had to abandon the idea of ever becoming a pro player. I knew that eSports was going to be big. It was inevitable, but even though I was only twenty-one, I didn't want to wait around for it to catch on. I was already too old, and I didn't want to be a player forever. It felt like I missed my window to do that.

Instead, I refocused all of my energy into figuring out how to use my skill set to become a part of this next big thing, but I still didn't know how. Okay, I could do video content. Maybe I could be a talk-show host. How about a commentator? Yeah, I'd be interested in all those options, but they weren't careers. I didn't have that answer yet. My mother always told me that if I wanted to do this for a living I had to make sure I was properly channeling my efforts. This meant getting myself out there, even if I wasn't making any money at first. I had to start somewhere and that's why I refereed GameBattles matches online. I thought GameBattles was such a great place for gamers to showcase their ability and I wanted to be a part of that any way I could.

This was how I became affiliated with MLG. I really liked what MLG was trying to do with eSports. So in 2008, when I heard there was going to be an event nearby in Columbus, I immediately volunteered to be a *Halo* referee. I wasn't getting paid, but I could network and I ended up making great connections. I was still in school and just doing this for fun. I never pictured in a million years that things would turn out the way they did. MLG made me a part-time contractor, so during the week I'd run the GameBattles online tournament system. There would be like six to twelve tournaments over the weekend, and I could make anything from a couple hundred to a couple thousand dollars. My job was to make sure the tournaments were organized and running properly so they would generate revenue for MLG. When it came time for events, they would contract me to fly out and officiate *Halo* stations. These events were all about *Halo*. *Call of Duty* was like the elephant in the room that nobody wanted to address.

I liked the idea of possibly commentating, but the opportunity had never presented itself for *Call of Duty*. I tried pushing for it, but MLG didn't seem interested. Chris Puckett was such a dominant personality in *Halo*. I didn't want to simply stand in his shadow and be "that other *Halo* commentator." I was a *Call of Duty* player. I loved *Call of Duty*. As much as I liked to play *Halo*, *Call of Duty* was my game. When I looked at the amount of activity on GameBattles I realized that people were playing online *Call of Duty* tournaments. They weren't playing online *Halo* tournaments. It was no surprise that *Call of Duty 4* was becoming the game of the year in 2009.

Finally, at the 2009 MLG National Championships in Anaheim, I got my first shot at commentating. I was reffing *Halo* stations when the tournament organizers came up to me and said they planned to add the *Call of Duty* finals to the end of the broadcast if there was enough time. They asked me if I wanted to commentate. "Absolutely!" I did have some experience. As we had been gearing up to do GameBattles live, I had commentated some recorded *Call of Duty* matches while we were trying to figure out the pilot program. These were all done in my bedroom, but I had never commentated a live event with people watching. This would be the first.

I always thought it would be amazing to go up there on the main stage in front of a crowd at an MLG event. I looked at this as my opportunity to forge new ground. Why couldn't I be to *Call of Duty* what Puckett was to *Halo* and what Day[9] was to *Starcraft*? I was confident, maybe even borderline arrogant, that I could be great at this. I knew the game well enough, and I felt that I had the right personality so I could break the mold of what a cliché gamer was to those outside the industry. This could turn into something. I didn't know what, but there was definitely an opportunity here.

There I was backstage at the venue in Anaheim and it looked like that opportunity was going to slip through my fingers. It all came down to there being enough time, and sure enough, the semifinal match between Fear and EnVy started to run long. They were playing a game mode called *Sabotage,* but time kept expiring and they had to keep playing until they had a winner. *Of course it couldn't be this easy.* There was nothing I could do but sit and watch. At this point, I wish they never even asked me. I was about to give up hope when the match finally ended. EnVy won and was set to play Xtravagant in the finals. It turns out there was just enough time, so everything worked out perfectly.

The finals started. EnVy vs. Xtravagant for the 2009 *Call of Duty* Championships and I was commentating my first-ever event. I don't think I will ever forget this experience as long as I live. The stage may have been different, but I kept telling myself that it was the same thing I had been doing at home in my bedroom. I tried to paint the picture while doing play-by-play and color. Once I got in the zone, I realized it was the exact same thing. The actual play-by-play may be the same, but there was something about doing it in person and in front of a camera during a live television moment that leaves no room for error. That was definitely nerve-racking and like nothing I had ever experienced before. There was a lot to this job that took some getting used to—like being all buttoned up and doing a live pregame show with no teleprompter while potential sponsorship opportunities were on the line. That was challenging, but the only way I got better was with real commentating experience at live LAN events.

I wish I could tell you more, or if I learned anything from this first experience, but I never went back and listened to myself commentate the event. I make it a point to never listen to any of the matches I commentate. I don't think I've heard myself talk for more than five minutes. I can't stand the sound of my own voice—which is ironic because I talk so much. I shouldn't say never. There was one time, right before the *Black Ops 2* Championship a couple years later, when I went back and watched a game play that I commentated for *Call of Duty 4*. Before hearing that, I would've told you that once you get in the rhythm you hit your stride and it's all the same, but I could tell what a substantial improvement I had made as a commentator over the past three or four years. I may not have recognized it until that moment, but the repetition allowed me to get a lot better over time. I probably would have benefited from going back and listening to old matches, but I was so appalled after hearing my own voice that it reaffirmed my initial reasons for not wanting to listen to myself.

It was after the 2009 National Championship that I became a *Call of Duty* commentator. I had played a ton of *League of Legends*. I've played *Dota*. I could definitely cast another game, but I focused on *Call of Duty* because I loved the game and I had fun doing it. It was my game and I would be its commentator. I could feel the shift getting ready to occur. Here was this franchise starting to gain a lot of attention.

5

BACK TO OUR ROOTS

H3CZ

With more money coming in than ever, and our fan base rapidly expanding by the end of 2010, we decided to go back to our roots and reinvest in competitive eSports. I thought it was an interesting idea, but some of the other snipers on the team like DTreats and Predator were like, "No way. We're a sniper team. We make videos on YouTube. We're not a part of that world." They thought they had something good and didn't want to go messing with eSports. I could see where they were coming from, but at the same time I wanted to grow and that meant venturing into competitive *Call of Duty*. Had I been a pushover and just said, "You know what, you guys are my stars, so I'm not going to risk upsetting you," who knows where OpTic and all of competitive *Call of Duty* would be today. The snipers weren't going anywhere. They still had their team, but OpTic was also going to have a competitive team.

We didn't exactly hit the ground running. Our first attempt was a disaster. We had been talking with Machinima about creating a tournament for competitive *Call of Duty* and this was how Frag Cup was

born. Since Machinima was hosting and OpTic had some of their premier directors, we wanted to make sure that we had a really good
competitive team. The squad we put together consisted of me, Di3seL,
Nerve, and Gunner.

Going in, we thought we were good, but trying to get back into
the competitive scene after taking such a long break was a mistake.
We had been so heavily focused on one weapon that we didn't know
the ins and outs, or what was common knowledge among the players. We had a lot of backing from our fans, who wanted to see us
win, but the outcome was pretty sad.

I always wanted to be a pro and thought of as one of the best.
I've always been a competitive person. Even if it was an argument, I
wanted to win. This tournament made me realize that I didn't have
what it takes. Some people have it. Some don't. In the end, it's a God-
given talent. You can train harder and practice longer than anyone
and might never become a pro. I didn't have it, but I knew that I could
still be involved.

My original thinking was this: Who were the biggest names in
Call of Duty? At the time, they were personalities and most of them
were on OpTic. We weren't on the eSports side yet, but we were large
enough to say that if we started a team and decided to sell T-shirts, we
would sell more shirts than every other team combined. So instead
of taking the already established YouTubers on OpTic and trying to
turn them into professional players, why not do the opposite? We
would hire professional players and then teach them to be YouTubers.
It was like an aha moment. When a door shuts, another one opens. If I
couldn't be the best player, I was going to own the best organization. I
asked Di3seL to go out and find the top players in the competitive *Call
of Duty* community.

At this stage, it wasn't even about winning. We wanted to win,
but that's not what mattered most to me. I knew that if I wanted to
build a successful team, the foundation had to be fandom. The fans
mattered. I knew what it was like to be a fan. I was just like so many
others out there who were nerds when it came to *Call of Duty*. Being

one of them, I knew what they wanted. We had to build a champion-ship fan base before we built a championship team.

Putting together the team was actually quite easy. When it came to recruiting the players, I completely trusted in Di3seL, and the play-ers he found to make up our first competitive roster were MerK, Flaw-less, Vengeance, and a scrawny little kid called NaDeSHoT. OpTic had over three hundred thousand subscribers, so our pitch was simple. "We can put you in front of as many eyeballs as possible, and help you not only to create content, but teach you how to profit from that content." It didn't take much convincing because up to that point, *Call of Duty* to them was the chance to win a couple hundred dollars each, and that's only if they came in first at an event. When I showed them my recent PayPal deposits from Machinima to prove that the money I was making off videos was legit, they saw the light. There was now a way to make money off video games other than competing. They said yes right away.

Normally, at MLG events the teams wear T-shirts for uniforms, so we decided to take this to the next level and go with paintball jer-seys. This way we could stick with the first-person shooter theme without having to resort to camouflage or an army uniform. Right at the beginning we made a rule that only the pros can wear the white jerseys and we'd sell the black jerseys for everyone else. I couldn't even wear a white jersey because I wasn't a pro player. Looking back at it now, these weren't the best-looking jerseys, but they were different and helped us stand out. It worked and people could recognize our team from a mile away. This was our attempt to take a Jordan-like approach to merchandising. Even at the very beginning I planned on retiring that jersey after every season so you could never buy that par-ticular jersey again. This way we would have new jerseys every year.

In November of 2010, OpTic entered its first professional tourna-ment at MLG Dallas. We now had to get the team there. We had spon-sors that could help out. SteelSeries would give us $400 per event, but each event cost about $4,000. Back then, the sponsors didn't really get what we were creating. Even today, a lot of companies don't fully understand the power of social media. There was no immediate ROI (return on investment) to justify spending all of this extra money on this new unproven thing. So for this tournament the players had to pay for their own travel, but we would pick up everything else. And for that, all the members of OpTic volunteered 10 percent of their earnings to cover expenses. Not everybody was profiting from the team the way I was, so I put up the most. It was my team, so it would be my risk, but this was a way to involve the other members by giving them a sense of ownership in the team.

What made things more complicated for me personally was that I had just gotten in the clear with Judith. After quitting my job and going very far out on a limb, I finally proved to her that I could turn a profit. We were now making money, but here I was spending that money on a brand-new business venture. I couldn't guarantee that it would pan out, but just like I did when I started the company, I felt something. I knew that if we refocused our efforts and duplicated what we had learned as YouTubers, we could have that same success in eSports. I was so confident that I didn't even have a backup plan. This was going to work. Period. There was no other thought in my head. Failure wasn't an option.

PART 2

BUILDING A
PRO TEAM

MLG DALLAS 2010

NaDeSHoT

One day in the summer of 2010 I got this random message in the GameBattles forum from a guy named OpTic Nerve. He asked me if I wanted to be the captain of their competitive team. Not only had I never been approached like that before, but I had no idea what OpTic was. I was intrigued, so I hopped on a Skype call with Nerve, Hector, OpTicJ, and Di3seL. They talked about starting a competitive team and also the opportunity to make more formal YouTube videos for their channel.

I knew nothing about the sniping scene. I didn't know it even existed or that people could make a living off YouTube videos. I was uploading short *Call of Duty* highlights to my YouTube channel at the time, but I was oblivious to the fact that there was this huge community out there. Playing on the competitive team sounded great, but I really liked the idea of being able to make playing video games a job. To me that would be the best thing in the world. I never thought that was even possible. For a kid who only saw a couple hundred dollars here and there from tournament winnings, this was a whole new world.

What's funny is that everything I've ever accomplished over the course of my career as a pro player and on YouTube is mostly because of a game that I absolutely hated the first time I played it. When I got the Xbox in 2007, it came with *Call of Duty 2*. I signed on and then got spawn-trapped for the first ten minutes and never played it again. *Halo* was my game and I was obsessed. I'd come home from school, play *Halo 2* until I went to bed, and then wake up and do the same thing all over again. I also took an interest in *Gears of War* and that was the first game I played on LAN. It was at an MLG event in Chicago during my freshman year. I got to leave school early and came so incredibly close to placing in the top sixteen, which was all I wanted to do, but we fell just short and it was heartbreaking.

Later that year, all my friends in school were talking about *Call of Duty 4*. They convinced me to give the series another try and my parents got it for me at Christmas. This was a completely different experience for me. *Call of Duty 4* was just so competitive. I don't even think they meant to make it that competitive, but it turned out to be the best first-person shooter, right up there with *Halo 2*.

I had been playing with different teams on GameBattles and that's where I first met Joey Deluca, or MerK. We both went pro together and had a team called Sour Gummy Worms. We were just screwing around. We never expected anything to come of it, but we ended up placing in the top eight of a tournament and earned our pro label. It was during *Modern Warfare 2* that we were both approached by Nerve to join OpTic and we jumped at the opportunity.

The idea was for OpTic to enter a team at MLG Dallas in November 2010. The tournament was coming up, and MerK and I had enough pro points to qualify a team, but we couldn't find two more players because most of the other rosters were already set.

There was also this big switch going on at the time. All competitive *Call of Duty* up to that point was played on Xbox 360. Then MLG partnered with Sony and PlayStation, so they merged the communi-

GAMER TAG TALES

Since I was a *Halo* player before I was a *Call of Duty* player, it makes sense that my gamer tag originates with *Halo*. As you probably know, in the game, you could hit someone with a grenade to bring their shields down and shoot them once in the head and you'd get a kill, hence . . . NaDeSHoT. I am ashamed to say that I did steal the gamer tag from one of my old teammates on *Halo*. When he quit, I jacked the name and have been going by NaDeSHoT ever since.

ties. PlayStation had its own community of gamers, but they weren't mainstream or connected to the Xbox 360. They were like two separate bodies. All of the Xbox North American players had found teams already, so MerK and I were in a tough position. We needed to do something bold and decided to take the best PlayStation players and hope that we all worked well together. We didn't want to go to the event to be a crappy Xbox team. We wanted to win, so we sought out the best, and that's how we found Flawless and Vengeance. It was risky, but they turned out to be great. We now had a team, but we only had a month to practice before Dallas.

What made things hard for me was that I was still going to school. So there I was trying to make videos and practice with this new competitive team in the few hours I had after school. We were able to get in some time playing together during the PCL ladders prior to the tournament. Those ladders were basically like the regular season for the NFL or NBA, where you play all the other teams a few times. The records would determine the seeding for Dallas, which was like the Super Bowl or NBA Finals. Other teams had been practicing for months, but our team was kind of thrown together at the last minute, so I was nervous going in. I had no idea how any of this would pan out.

MLG Dallas was the first time I ever got to meet any of my teammates in person. MerK, Vengeance, Flawless, Hector, J, Tumors, Di3seL, and Nerve were all there. It was fun meeting everyone. They were all just as funny as they were online and during Skype calls. We hung out and could shoot the shit. The whole tournament was a blast. Tumors and Hector were two of the funniest guys I ever met. J was down-to-earth and really nice. Di3seL was this great, fun guy who was trustworthy and somebody you could talk to.

Still, I had to play and I was really nervous because this was a big deal. I was doing my best to stay on this team. Deep down inside I knew that I wasn't the best player out there, but I did know how to win and that's what they wanted. I just had to prove it. I have no idea why, but Nerve put a tremendous amount of pressure on me. He had a weird sense of humor and was kind of being an ass. Before the event even started, he was making these threatening jokes that I'd be off the team if I didn't place well. I already felt a ton of pressure, so this just sent my anxiety through the roof.

When it came time to play, this tournament was nothing like I had ever experienced before. I immediately knew that this was something I wanted to do and an organization I wanted to be a part of for a very long time. Our very first match was against EnVyUs, who were the heavy favorites going in. They had been absolutely destroying every-body on the pro circuit, and naturally we had to draw them right off the bat. This was a huge challenge and really the only one that mattered because if we beat them, we knew we had a good chance of winning the event. They had two of the best players in StaiNViLLe and ProoFy. Nobody wanted to play EnVyUs.

It was nerve-racking the whole time, but we took them down 3–1 in a best of five. That win was the most incredible feeling, but I also had to pee the entire time. Whenever I'm really nervous and I've had a lot of caffeine, I always have to pee. No matter what the tournament, I have to pee before every match. I really have to pee after every map, but I can't do that at an event. It almost feels like going to a movie and having to hold it in because you don't want to miss anything.

It was so extreme and for a while I thought I had to go to a doctor.

We were so stoked after beating EnVyUs, but from there things started to go downhill. We kind of just fell apart later in the weekend. We didn't catch any breaks and weren't getting lucky. It was a domino effect. We started losing, and before we knew it, we had gotten knocked out by Xtravagant. It was an eight-team event and we placed fourth, but we played very well even though the outcome didn't really reflect it. It was weird because my emotions were just so up and down that whole weekend. I was terrified going in, but that nervousness turned into this absolute elation after we beat EnVyUs. That didn't last long and it taught me never to get too comfortable because things can change so quickly.

I learned so much that weekend. Now I had proved that I could play at this level and perform well as a captain. I always had confidence in myself, but there's a big difference between knowing that you can compete with the best and then showing everyone else. The fourth-place finish was disappointing because I was really hoping for a top-three finish if not a win. As I learned throughout the years, you can't win 'em all.

THE STORY BEHIND THE GREEN WALL

The term "Green Wall" was coined at our first tournament in Dallas. Standing behind the players on the team were me, my brother, OpTicJ, Di3seL, and Nerve. We were all big guys—much bigger than all these little teens walking around. Somebody shouted, "It's like there's a big green wall behind them." I want to say it was Paul "eGo" Megna who first said it, but I can't be sure. That was the first time we heard the term mentioned and we just ran with it.

—H3CZ

While still at the event, MerK and I decided to drop Vengeance and Flawless. We approached SidRoC and JKap—two of the players who just beat us on Xtravagant. The idea was for them to play with us on OpTic for the upcoming *Black Ops 1* season. We thought they were both incredible players and it was the best way for us to improve as a team. We brought them to the hotel room and Hector pitched them just like he did us: "Listen, if you guys want to have a future in competitive gaming, joining OpTic is one of the only ways you can accomplish that goal." We wanted to show them that you could make money off of YouTube. This was something that very few pro players realized at the time. You had to make yourself unique compared to everyone else. You had to build a following. You had to give people a reason to like you so fans would watch your streams and watch your videos. This would eventually allow you to make more money.

Now we had SidRoC and JKap. I was stoked from the very beginning and I knew we had one of the best teams going in to *Black Ops 1*. This was going to be the first season where they were going to have live events every month on the MLG pro circuit. This was a huge opportunity and we had to make it work. We all knew that this was when competitive *Call of Duty* was going to break and we were going to get our chance to shine on the pro circuit. *Call of Duty* was going to be right up there with *Halo*.

Black Ops 1 came out. The game was great. Everything fell into place, but then it kind of fell right out of place just as quickly. The problem was that SidRoC was an older guy and he had a full-time job, so he wasn't always able to practice. Right when a game comes out is the most crucial time of the year because it's when everyone needs to learn the game. This is the grind when you pick up on the spawns, rotations, and timing all while learning to play as one cohesive unit. There are nuances in a new game that didn't exist in the last one, so those are the things you need to pick up. Constantly practicing is the only way to do it. You have to come up with strategies and figure out the best way for your team to win. What type of maps can you push without spawning the other team out? There are so many intricate things about the game that you have to learn, but we weren't able to do that because SidRoC couldn't be relied on to make it to practice.

We parted ways with SidRoC and then JKap left with him. What MerK and I ended up doing was picking up two of their former teammates, Rambo and BigTymeR. It was risky, but we were confident that it would work out. BigTymeR and Rambo had won the *Call of Duty 4* National Championships in 2009, so we knew what they could do. We'd now added two powerhouse players in the game to our roster, but it takes more than talent to put together a good team. Unfortunately, Rambo and I would butt heads constantly. We were both these vocal leaders and both hardheaded, so that led to a lot of arguments. It was tough to have two guys like this on the team, but we fought through it and still played very well. At the beginning of *Black Ops 1* we were beating everyone online.

Everything changed for me one weekend when I was grounded by Mom. I don't even remember what I did, but she just got so sick of me playing video games and not coming out of my room, so she took away my Xbox. I tried to save face and cover for myself, so I lied to the rest of the team. I told them I had to go to my grandparents, and couldn't get online. Later that same night, I got a call from Hector saying that all three of the players wanted me off. They were going to pick up JKap. My heart sank. I was crushed. I had been so excited to be a part of this team and I could be one of the best. I was committed and wanted more than anything to make this happen. Then one day it all slipped right through my fingers.

MY FIRST REALLY TOUGH DECISION

H3CZ

There's never been a player on my team who I haven't taken an interest in personally. I always felt like a big brother to everyone on OpTic. That meant being there for the good and the bad. Now I was in a position where I had to break the news to NaDeSHoT that he had just been dropped by his own teammates. I felt terrible. I had just hung out with him the entire weekend in Dallas. This was the first time I had met him in person, but I could immediately tell that he wanted to do this. He was driven and determined to make a future out of *Call of Duty* just like I was. Now I had to crush that dream.

It's not like he played poorly that weekend. The thing with NaDe-SHoT was that he always caught a bad rap for not being good. The reason for that was because he was the guy on the team doing all the dirty work that nobody else wanted to do. That stuff was important, but at the end of the game he would still be the one with the least amount of kills. Unfortunately, sometimes that was what people remembered.

I had final say when it came to the makeup of the team, but I'm not on the front lines with the players. If they tell me something isn't working out, I'm going to believe them because they're the ones going through it. When MerK approached me about dropping NaDeSHoT to pick up some of the guys from Xtravagant, I had to trust his judgment. This was a direction we needed to take the team if we were going to be the best. *Call of Duty* was the Wild West back then. I didn't have contracts with my players. We were doing something new and it was working, but unfortunately this came with some cutthroat realities.

Nothing about this felt right. I told NaDeSHoT, "Hey, man, this is the deal right here. They want to drop you. It's better for the team at this point in time if we do it, but I still want you to be a part of OpTic. Forget about competing for the time being and just focus on YouTube. I want to teach you how to be a YouTube personality." I decided right there that I was going to take this little kid under my wing. I was going to be his mentor and protector. I told him that consistency was going to get him views, but the way to get the fans attached was for him to open up.

In NaDeSHoT I saw an introverted kid. He had this voice that was raspy and shrieky at the same time, but it was different. He was shy and nerdy, so he just looked like somebody's little cousin. I instantly knew that fans would attach themselves to him if we could get him to come out of his shell, so my goal from the get-go was to bring out his personality. We were going to give him a platform to be himself. I had already put him in front of the camera. We did a day-in-the-life behind-the-scenes-type interview thing in Dallas. It was much less formal than what we do now, but the idea was to show what we did at events. Right away I could tell he was nervous and that it was going to be difficult because he didn't get it right away, but that potential was there.

"Don't be embarrassed about who you are. You're a nerd? Embrace it. You aren't the coolest kid in school? Embrace it. You don't have a lot of friends? Embrace it." And that's something we still try to do today: we consider the fans friends we've never met. "If you get ten thousand people watching your videos, I guarantee that the majority of them will relate to you if for no other reason than because you both play video games. Maybe some of these people watching are introverts just like you are. Maybe they're shy and don't have that many friends either. They could see that you're doing this and think they can do it too. Be yourself and share your story. People will relate."

NaDeSHoT was going to be the guinea pig for my vision. I wanted to advertise him and make him a star. Luckily he was on board. This is when we started to realize his commitment to the team. What he was doing was not easy. He had a full-time job and was also going to school. It was tough on him and he was working harder than anyone else because after school and work he'd come home and make videos. So when he came back to me later that year looking to compete again, we created a second OpTic team for him called OpTic Nation. This when he started to come in to his own. He was now in charge of this team and put a good group of players around him. OpTic Nation created that comfort level where he knew he wasn't going to be dropped.

We weren't profiting financially from the team when it came to eSports, but the way we were benefiting was much more valuable. I began to notice how the fans who weren't traditional eSports fans were taking more of an interest in the scene. Everyone was able to feed off this and it led to crossover collaborations. NaDeSHoT would make videos with the snipers. This exposed each of them to a different fan base. The fans of the snipers were introduced to NaDeSHoT while the eSports fans who followed him were exposed to the sniper videos. I know NaDeSHoT witnessed a huge spike in subscribers—I believe he gained four thousand in one day after doing one of these collaborations. Predator and NaDeSHoT worked so well together that they created a very successful series called *Snipers Going HAM* that gained traction and found an audience. In typical NaDeSHoT fashion, he took the ball and ran with it.

Consistently producing content and collaborating with other members on all sorts of different projects was what helped NaDeSHoT grow. No other eSports players were doing this at the time. You either did YouTube or you played eSports. NaDeSHoT was the first to combine the two. This helped boost his popularity and that of the OpTic eSports team. When we'd show up at a tournament with NaDeSHoT on our roster, people knew who he was. He had fans and supporters who were rooting for him because they all felt like they knew him personally after watching him on YouTube. They didn't know the players on the other teams as well as they knew NaDeSHoT and OpTic. This was powerful and helped take us to the next level.

H3CZ'S TOP-THREE TOURNAMENT EXPERIENCES

MLG Dallas 2010 was huge for us because we played well and made our mark on the scene immediately. That's why it will always be tops on my list of favorite tournaments. After Dallas, I'd go with our first-ever tournament win in 2011, which solidified us as a team and proved that we could make that happen. I'm going to round out the list with X Games because it was the first time *Call of Duty* was featured outside its normal realm. It was the first time eSports were featured alongside other sports. I would have said *CoD* XP, which was huge for OpTic, but it was more of a circus exhibition than it was an actual competition.

1. MLG Dallas 2010
2. MLG Columbus 2011
3. X Games 2014

We were about to make waves on the competitive scene, and that scene was growing. So was OpTic. Before Dallas, we had never played at an MLG event, but the moment we stepped into that venue at the Hilton Anatole, we were fan favorites. I suddenly had fifteen people standing around me asking for pictures and autographs. It was weird. Having that connection with strangers was electric. Once we put the name OpTic on the back of our players' jerseys, fans immediately attached themselves to our team. It's funny because even though we were the most popular team, we were still the underdog. Who doesn't root for the underdog? It hit me right away: *Holy crap, we're gonna be huge.*

It was also in Dallas where I met Fwiz for the first time in person. We had communicated through Twitter, but had never met. I was at a private party when I went up to him and said, "Hey, man, you said online you were going to give me VIP. What's up?" He just laughed and kept walking. Later on we took a picture together and exchanged information so we could keep in touch. He was funny and a really fast talker. This was a guy who could talk his way into absolutely anywhere. We got along immediately. I could sit and talk with him about the industry for hours. It wasn't long before I asked him to join OpTic as our eSports manager.

THE BEST YEAR OF MY LIFE

Fwiz

immediately wanted to talk to Hector because I thought this was an opportunity where we could both help each other a lot. He wanted to get into eSports because, just like myself, he could tell that this thing was going to be big. It was a no-brainer. Here was a great opportunity. Pairing what Hector was doing with OpTic up with eSports was a match made in heaven. What made us work so well together was that we just got along and had similar personalities. I mean the guy is still one of my best friends.

The conversation Hector and I had was pretty simple. Here was OpTic Gaming, which had gained traction as these pub snipers who did cool tricks and entertained people on YouTube. Here was me, who was on the rise and really the only commentator for *Call of Duty* making any kind of noise in this market. I had not been involved on the YouTube side at all, but I understood how big that was and could become. I looked at it more as a business merger. We pooled our resources and worked toward achieving one objective. And while doing all this, I could still commentate over OpTic game play and help put gaming content on their YouTube channel. It would be good for my visibility and help me earn cash as well. It was mutually beneficial. So in 2010 we decided to team up and just take over the scene. OpTic was becoming the quintessential brand for everything that's cool about being a gamer. We wanted to break the stigma. It was more of a lifestyle and I still think it is to this day.

The scene was ready to explode, but there was one major problem. None of these *Call of Duty* tournaments at this point were traditional LAN events. They were all held online until we got down to the final eight, and then MLG would host a once-a-year event. Unlike a traditional local area network, they had to run one Internet connection through Xbox Live in the venue. Running an Internet connection in a venue is really expensive. A game like *Halo* had a full-blown LAN, so they could have like two hundred teams. *Call of Duty* wasn't there yet.

This made qualifying a nightmare. You didn't ever want to play this type of high-level competition online because players could get kicked off. Some players had better Internet than others. A lot also depended on where you were hosting the game. If you were hosting on the West Coast, you'd be screwing players on the East Coast. Whenever there were thousands of dollars at stake, everyone had a reason to get pissed off about something and tempers flared. There was a constant competitive disadvantage because of the Internet.

Call of Duty couldn't be at a traditional MLG event because the game publisher was not putting the functions in the game to make that possible. I kept pushing Activision to put these eSports functions into the game, but in all fairness to them, eSports was still very small at the time. Putting engineering resources into making a LAN mode meant that you had to sacrifice other things in the game. All the people in the community, myself included, didn't have a complete understanding of what those other things were. All we knew was that they weren't there and because of it we couldn't play on LAN.

The other thing to consider was that the game went to a different publisher each year and not all of the publishers had the same attitude toward eSports. Infinity Ward had published *Call of Duty 4* and, to their credit, had just made it a huge hit. I think they were still trying to figure it all out and wrap their heads around what they had. That's why I don't ever discredit or get too frustrated with them because I sympathized with their situation. If I were in their shoes, I don't know if I would have wasted the resources or manpower at that time to create LAN capabilities simply because eSports wasn't that big yet. The younger version of myself would be absolutely furious to hear me say that right now, but the game was still in its infancy. There weren't even a lot of people who played the game before *Call of Duty 4*, so how would they even know to take that risk?

Everything changed with *Black Ops 1,* which was published by Treyarch. A few months before the November 2010 release of the game, I was invited by Treyarch to go to the multiplayer reveal event in Santa Monica. It was more like this huge party. Metallica played and celebrities like Kobe Bryant were there. The event was part of the *Call of Duty* Endowment, which was one of the company's great efforts to employ veterans. They decided to have the veterans play some grudge matches to show off the game. They asked me and HastrO, who was a former player and one of my early casting partners, to commentate matches where they pitted army vets against the navy guys. It was great because we got to see the game and meet a ton of people.

The game was phenomenal and it definitely had the eSports features the community had been waiting for. We could finally have two teams playing on a local network at the same time. The problem was that the timer in the lobby was much too short, so by the time all the players finally joined, they could be thirty-five seconds into a match. There was no lobby mode and this didn't allow players to get into a room, decide the map and mode, and then start as a collective group. In order to host a large-scale LAN event, we would need to have refs at every station to make sure both teams could fully join in the game. That just wasn't viable.

One of the people I met at the event was David Vonderhaar, who was the lead designer for the multiplayer experience. Afterward, HastrO and I told him, "David, this is really cool, but we need a LAN lobby because we can't get the players into the room in time to start the match and make it official." They obviously couldn't just rebuild the lobby mode because that was intensive and required a lot of resources. With only a couple weeks before the release of the game, David and his team were able to come up with an alternative to get around the problem by extending the countdown time in the lobby. Now everyone would have enough time to get into the game.

Black Ops 1 would be the first game in *Call of Duty* that could be played on LAN. You didn't need an Internet connection; you just needed to run Ethernet cable through the Xboxes and you could host a tournament with hundreds and hundreds of teams. This was the pivotal moment when competitive *Call of Duty* hit its stride. People could now come down to watch teams compete. This resulted in way more fan appeal. Because of that conversation HastrO and I had with David Vonderhaar in Santa Monica, we were able to change where *Call of Duty* was going as an eSport. For the 2011 season, *Black Ops 1* was put on the Major League Gaming circuit. There were seven major *Call of Duty* tournaments that year, and I commentated all seven of them. I was about to blow up.

My entire life changed in 2011. I was on fire, and looking back at it now, I think of it as one of the best years of my life. This was also the year when I landed that elusive full-time job in gaming that I had been searching for. For that, I credit OpTic. A few years earlier, Hector had helped Ryan Musselman land a job at Machinima. In January 2011, Ryan and Hector vouched for me when Machinima was looking for a community manager with a *Call of Duty* background. OpTic was a big creator for Machinima, so they had a lot of pull. I had the experience and felt overqualified for the position, but I don't think I would have gotten that job if OpTicJ and Hector didn't vouch for me and convince them that I was the right fit. I was so excited. I had been around gaming for so long, but this could lead to a career doing what I love. There was no way that I was going to squander this opportunity.

At Machinima, I was working with all of our different creators who were putting content on the channel. I worked to develop that content and then collaborated with the sales team to figure out how to sell it. I was one of the first couple of guys to start signing YouTube creators and partners to the platform so they could make money off the content on their YouTube channels. This whole gaming ecosystem was still in its nascent stages, but you could just tell that it was about to blow up quickly. There would be so many more opportunities on the horizon to forge new paths and make a name for myself internally and externally.

OpTicJ lived in L.A. with Di3seL, who also worked at Machinima. They shared an apartment, but their lease was up in January 2011, so we all decided to go in on a three-bedroom apartment in Burbank. We were broke as hell, but that didn't matter. It was great. We were all doing something we loved during the day, and there we were liv-

FWIZ'S TOP-THREE CASTING EXPERIENCES

This is all pretty cut-and-dried. No mystery here. My all-time favorite event that I ever commentated was that first National Championship in Anaheim. It was the first time I did it live and that made it the most exciting moment of my commentating career. The second was at XP because of the massive scale of this event and that my boys at OpTic took home the $400K first prize. Finally, I gotta put *Call of Duty* Champs for *Advanced Warfare* on that list as well because that was the last event I ever commentated. All sentimental reasons I know, but they will always be my favorites.

1. 2009 *Call of Duty* National Championships
2. *Call of Duty* XP
3. 2015 *Call of Duty* National Championships

ing in Los Angeles. There were beautiful women and fun things to do everywhere, so we would go out and party on the weekends. It was more fun than college.

The absolute, hands-down best part of living with these guys was playing video games at night. *Black Ops 1* had just come out. We bought a couple tables from IKEA. I set up my gaming PC, a couple of Xboxes, and we turned the apartment into a gaming bachelor pad. The only difference between us and so many other gamers out there was that thousands of people were watching us play.

A few years earlier I started live-streaming on Justin.tv so people could watch me play online. I paid to upgrade my Internet and bought a capture card—this all set me back a couple thousand bucks, which was a pretty significant investment for a college kid. I thought it was cool if even twenty people could hang out and watch me play. I could get my buddies to join, play a match, and then get some commentary from the people in the chat. Since I already had my channel and everything set up when I moved to Burbank, I was like, "Guys, let's just set up a LAN in the family room." We put my station on the far left next to the game capture so you could see all of us with the webcam and pick up our audio. Instead of just me streaming, we streamed all of us when we played. Nobody was doing this at the time. We were way ahead of the game.

That year I started with ten thousand subscribers and grew the channel to a hundred thousand. When Justin.tv was sold to Twitch, I was one of the first broadcasters partnered on Twitch, but I was never in it to just build this huge subscriber list. I had more fun playing video games when other people were watching and commenting on what I was doing. It added another level of engagement to something that was already incredibly engaging to begin with.

While doing all this, I could still commentate for MLG on the weekends. The bigger *Call of Duty* got, the more money I was getting per event and the more they were treating me like a star. Once again, I attribute this to my affiliation with OpTic Gaming. I think people generally liked me as a commentator, but OpTic gave me that extra bump. I had the OpTic team in my corner and they had a lot of fans who instantly became my fans. It was crazy, and it helped make me the biggest commentator in *Call of Duty* by far.

Finally things were happening, which was refreshing because people were beginning to doubt the future of *Call of Duty* eSports. I remember talking to one of the biggest players in the game back in 2010 during *Modern Warfare 2*, and even he was like, "Screw it. I'm done. I don't wanna do this eSports thing anymore. *Call of Duty* isn't taking eSports seriously, so why should I?" I was frustrated too, but I had more of an optimistic view on the whole thing. I told him, "Look, it's gonna get so big that they won't be able to ignore it. Even if they don't wanna acknowledge eSports right now, this thing is growing so fast that they're eventually gonna have to. Stick with it for a couple more years and see what happens."

That player was Will "BigTymeR" Johnson. I loved BigTymeR from day one. I first met him when he was in high school. He's always been a good guy and he's funny as hell. Good thing he did stick with it because not only did he find his way onto OpTic, but he made it into *The Guinness Book of World Records* as well.

ALL OF THIS ALMOST NEVER HAPPENED

BigTymeR

Yup, I was in the gaming version of *The Guinness Book of World Records* for winning thirteen *Call of Duty* titles and becoming the highest-earning player between 2009 and 2012. That record has now been completely blown out of the water by Crimsix, but still, it was pretty cool at the time.

Guinness actually found me on Twitter. A group of guys came to my tiny hometown in Arkansas to do a photo shoot. I think they were on a tour because after me they were headed to California for some *Mario Kart* player and then on to Washington for somebody else. We did the photo shoot in the woods. It took the entire day. I wanted to do something a little more low-key so it would better fit my personality, but they wanted this serious picture. They had me out there with assault rifles and looking real mean like a soldier. I don't know if I pulled that off, so the attempt to make it look serious is what ended up making it funny, so I guess everybody won.

I never thought that people would care enough about video games to feature me in a book like *Guinness*. Though I was a pretty arrogant kid, so I probably would have told you I'd be in the book for something. When I was fifteen, I kept telling my mom that I was going out to California to play in big tournaments and make all this money, but that didn't happen right away. I grew up right in the Bible Belt, where everyone was super conservative. I always knew growing up that I wanted to get out of the state and try new things. I really wanted to see how the world worked outside of my tiny town with a population of two thousand.

As a teenager, I played a lot of *Battlefield* online. I didn't know much of anything about MLG and I don't think it was big at the time, but there was one twelve-on-twelve *Battlefield* tournament they'd host every year. I was really good at the game and knew I had a shot, but trying to put together a team of twelve guys was pure chaos; still, we somehow managed to get organized enough to enter a team in the qualification tournament. We had to place in the top two to be invited out to California to compete for the $100,000 prize. That sounded big at first, but wasn't that big when you chop it up among eleven other guys. We ended up falling just short and placing fourth, so I didn't get to go then, but this was when the whole dream

GAMER TAG TALES

I actually stole my gamer tag. Back when I used to play *Battlefield 2* on PlayStation, there was a guy on one of the teams I played on called Big-Timer. Later, when I was playing doubles matches in *Halo* with my old friend and teammate Terrell, he wanted to be some sort of duo that had a cool name. He came up with LilTymer and wanted my name to be Big-TymeR, which he jacked from that guy back on *Battlefield*. I know it's super stupid, but I went with it. Terrell ended up quitting and not playing games anymore after that, but I stuck with BigTymeR.

started. It would take me a few more years before I would make it out to California.

My love of first-person shooters began way back in the day with *Medal of Honor* when I was a kid, and by high school I was really into *Halo*. It was my friend Brandon Thompson who first introduced me to *Call of Duty*. He let me borrow his copy of *CoD3*, and I played it for like a week to get used to the game. As soon as I started playing I just knew that I was way better than everyone else. I don't know what it was about that game, but it came naturally to me. *Call of Duty* 4 came out the following week and I picked that up right away.

Ray "Rambo" Lussier was involved in the *Call of Duty* scene before me. I first met Rambo back in 2004 when playing *Black Hawk Down* on PlayStation 2. We didn't even have microphones or headsets to talk to each other. It was all in-game chat, so I guess I didn't actually meet him then, but we were playing alongside each other back when the GameBattles website first started. It was called SoComBattles back then and they hosted some *Black Hawk Down* leagues. Fast-forward to high school and I'm playing a *Call of Duty* match on GameBattles with my friends when we went up against a team called EFX. I hear, "Holy shit, you're BigTymeR from *Black Hawk Down!*" It was Rambo. We sort of picked things up from there. I noticed he was on a much better team than me, so it was time to ditch my friends from high school and take it to the next level.

Rambo gave me my first shot when he invited me to join EFX. I don't even remember what the acronym stood for. Probably just a play on FX, but we played a shitload of matches. That's how I got my first real taste of competitive *Call of Duty*. We were something like two hundred and two hundred—we basically won half our matches on GameBattles. Maybe we were a little better than .500, but we definitely weren't great. I guess we were probably in the top ten or fifteen teams in the game. We didn't care about the record. All we wanted was the experience. There were certainly better teams out there. Teams like Unreal Talent, with some of the old-school *Call of Duty* legends like HastrO and Assassin, went like one hundred and zero and weren't dropping a match on GameBattles. We had played them. We were able to take maps off them and win at least one game in a series, so we knew we could compete.

Our leader was this guy named Corvette Mike. He was a funny guy and a good leader, but he wasn't all that great at the game. He's actually a poker pro now. I follow him on Twitter and saw him playing in the World Series of Poker not too long ago. Ray and I had fun playing with these guys on EFX, but we knew that if we teamed up with some of the top-tier players, we could have a shot at competing against a team like Unreal Talent. If we were going to take it seriously, we had to form the best team possible.

MLG finally announced that they would host three pro circuit ladders and an actual National Championship event at the end of the year in 2009. MLG was getting serious, so in the summer we decided to part ways with EFX and formed Xtravagant. We picked up Dodgers and Sharp to round out the roster. This was the first time we could win actual money, so we were stoked about that. This was around the time when I had just graduated high school. I was also playing baseball year-round. After we finished fourth in the first pro circuit ladder, I kind of turned my attention to baseball. To really compete in the ladders you needed to play eight hours a day and my team was getting flustered because I was choosing baseball. I ended up leaving Xtravagant and figured I'd just get ready for college. I had already accepted a scholarship to Arkansas State that fall and I didn't see much of a future in *Call of Duty*.

This was also the summer when my mom figured it was time for me to get some real-life work experience. I had never really worked before, so she enrolled me in this program called Work Force. So for the rest of the summer I did all kinds of jobs around town. One day I'd be at city hall checking water meters. I'd be sweeping the street the next day, and then weeding the railroad tracks the day after that. It was awful. Fuck that job! After working one day out in the 110-degree heat, I came home and was browsing the Internet when I saw the prize pool for the *Call of Duty* National Championship was $10,000 for first place. This got my attention.

After playing that first pro circuit ladder, I knew we had a legitimate shot at winning. It was at that moment that I knew I had to get back into *Call of Duty* if for no other reason than because I was not cut out for the manual labor lifestyle. It was an equal amount love affair with *Call of Duty* as it was a hate affair with regular work. I rejoined Xtravagant for the third pro circuit ladder. We didn't win any of the ladders, but we got enough points, and were consistent enough, to get the number one seed at the national tournament in Anaheim. We were stoked.

Our sponsor at the time was Paul Megna, who ran this company called Icons 360, and they were funding our hotel and travel for the event—that's why for that tournament we were going to be called Xtravagant Icons. It was perfect except for the fact that I couldn't fucking go. I was seventeen. When you grow up in Marked Tree, Arkansas, you don't do a lot of traveling. My dad always supported me with whatever I did, but my mom . . . eh . . . not so much. I always did well academically, so as long as I took care of that stuff she didn't see the harm in me playing video games. But traveling to California with a bunch of people I met online was a little different. My mom had never been outside the state of Arkansas, so if I was going to talk her into letting me go on this trip, it would take a lot of begging. I had to get Paul on the phone with my mom to help convince her that I wasn't going to get assaulted at some hotel. After weeks of begging, and with Paul's help, she finally said yes.

The 2009 *Call of Duty* National Championships in Anaheim was my first-ever LAN event. It was cool to be there, but let me tell you, it was weird as all hell. This was the first time any of us on the team had ever met each other in person. We didn't have Twitter back then, so we communicated through like the GameBattles forum. We were all these supercompetitive seventeen- and eighteen-year-old guys and there was ruthless shit-talking between the teams online. When we got to the tournament, it was hilarious to see what some of these keyboard warriors actually looked like and how different they were in real life. Now everyone had to come face-to-face with the people they've been ragging on all summer. It was definitely awkward at first, but as the tournament went on, and we actually saw how everyone else acted in real life, things settled down.

This was all way before *Call of Duty* got big, so MLG stuck us in a dark basement. Not really, but it felt like it. We were the *Call of Duty* kids who nobody liked because everyone there was a *Halo* fan. There were only eight teams invited to compete and it was a double elimination tournament, so we only had to win three games to take home the title. There were warm-up matches on the first day, but when the actual bracket play started, it went by really quick. We opened the tournament by breezing through the eighth seed, but that second match where we played a better team was pretty close. We won that match and made it to the finals, where we had to play EnVyUs for the second time in the tournament. This was when things got a little crazy.

The finals were on the MLG main stage, where all the *Halo* teams played. Lights were everywhere and shining down on us. They had an announcer come on named Farouk, and he introduced the teams. Everybody was watching. This was completely different from playing at home behind a screen online. It was extremely nerve-racking. The first map we played was a Search and Destroy on Backlot. Since you don't respawn, every life you have is extremely important. I was literally shaking uncontrollably when I spawned because I knew how important it was. I had never been thrown into that situation before with the lights in my face, people in the stands, and the commentators in the booth. It just felt like every single eye in the place was on me and they were all waiting for me to screw up. I couldn't stop shaking, but after that first game I got all the jitters out of my system and we just played some *Call of Duty*.

We won the tournament and took home $2,000 each. With that

BIGTYMER RANKS THE *CALL OF DUTY* TITLES

The game I had the most fun playing had to be the game we're talking about right now, *Call of Duty 4*. For sure. Probably all of the old-school players would tell you the same thing, but not because of the actual game. For me it's more because that was the first one I played competitively. I have a lot of memories and met a lot of friends while playing that game. This was the game I went to Nationals for. Probably after that, I'd say *Black Ops 1* because it was the first time I got to travel for an entire season. We were pretty successful and I loved that team. For that last spot I could go either *Modern Warfare 2* or *Black Ops 2,* but I'm going to go with *Black Ops 2.* That was a pretty fun year all around.

1. *Call of Duty 4*
2. *Black Ops 1*
3. *Black Ops 2*

money I upgraded my monitors and controllers. I bought my first pair of A40s. All that equipment is standard now, but back in 2009 people were playing on tube TVs and using their regular Xbox mic. More importantly, this tournament got me in good with my mom. If I didn't win that tournament, my life would be completely different today. My mom wanted me to focus on school, but that money was just barely enough to convince her that there might be some longevity in this *Call of Duty* thing.

The following year we were back in Dallas for the *Modern Warfare 2* National Championship. Rambo and I had replaced Dodgers and Sharp with JKap and SidRoC. We were good. I'm not just saying that. We were the best *Modern Warfare 2* team out there. I know I'm biased because I was on the team, but during pro circuit ladder two we won without even dropping a map. It was during that third pro circuit ladder when things came apart. I think I can trace it all back to one moment. Rambo is the kind of guy who will always tell you right to your face what you're doing wrong. We had just lost a match and he said something to SidRoC, and that didn't sit right with him. Now they weren't getting along and that tension poured over into the game. Once that happens, you're done. If you're not getting along outside the game, it's never going to work inside the game. We knew going into Dallas that it was probably the last time we were going to play with each other.

It was at this tournament that I had my first-ever encounter with OpTic Gaming. I didn't really know much about them before this. I wasn't big on YouTube, and honestly, the competitive community didn't pay much attention to the sniper thing. YouTube and streaming were very foreign to us. There were guys on the competitive side who were doing it, but most of my time was spent practicing and trying to win tournaments. That's all I really thought about. Now, in 2010, OpTic had a competitive team. It was NaDeSHoT, MerK, Flawless, and Vengeance. The *Call of Duty* community was tight back then, so we'd been playing with MerK and NaDeSHoT online for at least a year.

What was strange was that OpTic was the first team with real fans. It was all kind of intimidating. Our four guys from Xtravagant were standing across from OpTic, and behind their competitive team stood all these huge guys. It was H3CZ, OpTicJ, Di3seL, and H3CZ's brother, Tumors. You could tell they were really passionate about their team. They had uniforms with this paintball-inspired concept. I didn't even know how to approach them.

As expected, we didn't do well and neither did OpTic. I think we finished third and they finished fourth. After these big tournaments is when everyone talks about their team changes and who wants to leave their organization to form a God squad or whatever. Both our teams wanted to make a move. Originally MerK and NaDeSHoT picked up JKap and SidRoC, but that didn't work out for whatever reason and then they approached Rambo and me. We knew Xtravagant probably wouldn't be competing again, so joining OpTic seemed like a natural move.

H3CZ ON BIGTYMER

Will was considered one of the best players in the game. Picture the starting pitcher on the varsity baseball team in high school. BigTymeR was that guy. He was smart, funny, good-looking, and the guy that everybody wanted to be around. And he had this southern drawl that came out every so often and that made him seem so laid-back and down-to-earth. That's why people gravitated toward him. And when it came to *Call of Duty*, he was winning. He cared about winning and he knew how to win, but it was his in-game leadership that helped make him such a legendary player. He was the type of dude who remained cool and calm. It always seemed like he knew what to do, and that was something that put his teammates at ease. The decision to bring Will on board was an easy one.

Gaming was something I did just for fun. I planned on finishing school and getting a job. I had no idea how far this *Call of Duty* thing would go. There wasn't the kind of money involved where I could do this for a living, but I had played long enough to know we were the best in the world at this. There was something appealing about that regardless if we were getting paid or not. I enjoyed being able to say that I was better than everyone else at something.

Black Ops 1 came out at the end of 2010, and the OpTic roster was me, Rambo, JKap, and MerK. The way we all played together felt like second nature—it should because this was basically our same team from last year with MerK instead of SidRoC. Rambo was the guy who held it all together. He was known for being that leader who would keep us all in line. I'd go so far as to say that this *Black Ops 1* squad was probably one of my favorite teams that I've played on because of how fluid and easy everything was. And we got along outside of the game, which always helps.

We had success in 2011, but we also developed a rivalry with Leverage. Aches was their leader, and he had always been a solid player. We used to beat him during *Modern Warfare 2*, but you could always tell that he would never give up. He just kept talking shit on the forum, but he was a guy who could actually back it up, which made it even more infuriating. Leverage had another young kid in Scump. We didn't know much about him. He must have only been fifteen at the time, but we soon realized he was this young slayer who could give us some trouble if we weren't at the top of our game.

10

SOMETIMES YOU JUST GOTTA GET LUCKY

Scump

ood morning to all you gamers out there!

It might not be morning for you, but it's morning for me. Well, it's 1:30 P.M., but that's as close to morning as I get these days. Most gamers don't get up before noon anyway. We're trying something a little different here. This isn't a *Call of Duty* commentary or me blither-blabbering on my live stream. I'm going to give you the story behind the story and try to tell you guys some things that you might not know.

The question I get asked all the time is "Scump, how do I become a pro player?" I'll answer that one in a sec, but first I'm going to tell you my story and it involves a whole lot of timing and luck. MLG Dallas 2011 was the first tournament of the *Black Ops 1* season and my first tournament as a pro. I was playing for Leverage and was extremely lucky to win my first-ever pro tournament, which almost never happens, by the way, but my story goes way behind luck because one week before the event I wasn't even on Leverage.

I'm going to start at the beginning. No, that's a horrible idea. We're not starting at the beginning. Let's start in middle school. Specifically right before I became a pro player. I was playing *Halo* and *Halo 2* religiously. I also played a little bit of *Call of Duty 2,* but, eh . . . that wasn't a very sound game. The campaign was fun, but the online matchmaking couldn't even touch *Halo,* which was on a completely different level. I just got bored with *Call of Duty 2* because there was no replay value for me at all, so I went back to playing *Halo.*

Now *Call of Duty 4* was a completely different story. That matchmaking system was a lot of fun, and the multiplayer was much more competitive. This is what got my attention and made me want to play more. It was something new, and by that point I had been playing *Halo* so much that it was starting to get a little bit old anyway, so I switched over to *Call of Duty.* Me and my friends would come home from school and play 3v3 matches. We did this for like two years and it was a much more enjoyable experience than *Halo* ever was.

As soon as I discovered MLG and started to learn about players and tournaments, it immediately got my attention. I knew that this was something I wanted to do. What I really loved about gaming was the ability to stand out and earn a reputation for being a good player. I played football and baseball too, but I couldn't get nearly the same kind of exposure. On the GameBattles ladder there were over six thousand teams. If I could climb to the top of that ladder and get first, picture how many people would know who I was. That was cool to me, and the grind to constantly get better became my motivation. I wanted the pros to know my name. I wanted to get on a pro team, and out of all these thousands and thousands of people playing, I wanted to be known as the best.

It was on GameBattles that I first met Bob Hamwi. I was playing on a team with my high school friends and he was playing on a team with his high school friends. They played TDM (Team Deathmatch, which was actually much bigger back in the day) just like we did, but they were a lot better than us. It's so weird how all this happened because it would never happen today, but I sent them a message asking for a tryout. "Hey, you guys are really good. I'd like to try out for your team." Looking back on it, this whole tryout was a little dumb. I ended up 1v1-ing the leader of their clan in TDM on Kill Shack and beat him. It's a weird way to join a team, but they were like, "Okay, you're good. You're in."

Bobby and I started to mesh, and at the end of *Call of Duty 4* in 2009, we began playing competitively when the online pro leagues began. They were called PCLs and we started playing in the very last one for *Call of Duty 4*. It was like joining a tournament nowadays. Anybody could play. It didn't matter if you were a pro or not, but it came down to credits and we were able to play enough matches in the league to qualify. The top eight or sixteen teams were placed in a bracket and they played it out. We did well and our reputation continued to grow heading into *Modern Warfare 2* the following year. Bobby and I became really close friends after this, and we split off from that team with his high school friends to try to make a name for ourselves.

GAMER TAG TALES

My gamer tag used to be Kong08 because my dad was really into *King Kong*. Then back during *Call of Duty 4,* when I was about twelve, I was driving with my mom down the highway when I looked out the window and saw a billboard for a Cracker Barrel or Bob Evans–type restaurant. At the bottom, it read MMMM . . . SCRUMPTIOUS. I got the idea then to change my gamer tag to Scrump. I soon realized that it looked kind of weird, so I modified it slightly to Scump. Then, during *Modern Warfare 2,* I considered completely changing it to Skylight, but quickly went back to Scump and everyone was thankful for that. So, my gamer tag came out of nowhere. Literally. People started suggesting I add *ii*'s or a *y*, and that caught on for a while, though I'm trying to revert back to plain Scump and not Scumpii because I don't really like the two *ii*'s at the end.

He lived in nearby New Jersey, so we could travel together to play in local tournaments. This gave us the chance to play a bunch of pros and we always did very well in these tournaments. This is how we got noticed, and these tournaments played a big role in me getting to where I am today.

My mom and dad divorced when I was very young, and I was raised by my mom, but my dad lived close by. He was an athlete and I'd go to the gym with him five days a week to work out. No matter what the sport I was playing, I never wanted to lose to anybody. I had that killer instinct as long as I could remember. Our youth football team was undefeated for five years, so I've never been used to losing. It was always about doing whatever possible to make sure I won.

By the time I got to ninth grade I wasn't as passionate about sports as I used to be. The coaches would yell and put me down. I got that they were trying to get the best out of me, but it just wasn't fun anymore. The final straw came when I dislocated my elbow during freshman football practice. I was a running back, so I was constantly getting hit, but I didn't even know that anything was wrong until I got in the shower and one of my friends pointed it out. "What the hell happened to your elbow?" I looked down and saw that the bone was literally out of place. You'd think that I would have felt pain or at least sensed that something was wrong. It didn't hurt at all, but I was still freaked out because dislocating a bone had always been my biggest fear—even more than breaking a bone. They took me to the hospital and snapped my arm back into place. It wasn't as bad as I thought it was going to be, but it was still pretty damn bad.

I did not want to play sports anymore, but I didn't know how to tell my parents, especially my dad, because he was so heavy into sports. I mean, he was the number one pick in the 1984 MLB draft. A part of me was worried that they wouldn't let me quit, but I had to say something. About a week after that injury, I was riding home from the gym with my dad when I finally told him. "I can't do this anymore." He questioned me at first, but I told him that it wasn't fun. I didn't like going to the gym five times a week. I dropped this bomb on him, and to my surprise, he was super understanding about it all. "I'm not going to force you to play. Do what you want to do."

Not only was that a huge weight off my shoulders, but now my schedule was free. I had an extra two or three hours every day after school to do the one thing that I was really passionate about—gaming. And this couldn't have come at a better time because I was just starting to make a name for myself as an up-and-coming player. What I didn't realize at the time was that my mom thought I was depressed because I spent all day in my room screaming at people online. I did that a lot.

What people don't realize is how hard it is to get noticed. You can be so freakin' good at the game. You can be the best player in the world, but finding that opportunity to get to the next level requires a lot of patience. There is so much luck involved. You have to play your cards right and hope that things work out. Today there aren't nearly as many teams on GameBattles and people don't regard these matches like they did back in the day. In my opinion, it's probably five times harder to get recognized and go pro today than it was when I got started. Today you have to go to LAN tournaments and that's sort of the only way. You can play in online tournaments, but if you beat pros they're just gonna blame it on connections, or write somebody off as a warrior.

Once I started on GameBattles, it took me like two or three years to even get noticed and earn a shot with my first pro team. What I did was try to get my name out there by playing with pro players, and the best way to do that at the time was playing in the PCL ladders. You could play against pros every single time you got a match. On Game-Battles you never knew who you were going up against. It could be a mess-around squad. I wish those ladders were still around because they were a lot of fun. It was during one of the first PCL ladders on *Modern Warfare 2* in 2010 that I landed a spot on my first pro team.

I knew two of the players on Fear and they were looking for a fourth. They knew I was really good, and I had actually just teamed with them a few months earlier, so I approached them. Just by con-

SCUMP'S TIPS ON BECOMING A PRO PLAYER

The obvious way to get better is to grind the game. Play a lot because it takes time. Nobody becomes a good player overnight. You have to know the game you're playing inside and out. This also means making sure you have the right equipment. Get a Scuf controller and get a good headset. These things aren't cheap, but consider them an investment.

Playing a lot is important, but what's just as important is who you play with. You have to enjoy playing with the people on your team. If you're just beginning, start local and find a group of people at your school. As you go up the ranks try to move on to better and better teams. You want to make sure your teammates are reliable and have the same goals. To be the best you have to play with the best, but be careful because this doesn't necessarily mean picking teammates based only on skill. You want to consider factors like communication and how they are outside the game to make sure you get along. Every team needs players who can communicate and keep a level head. In the long run, that's more important than someone who goes out there looking for kills. Chemistry is crucial and the lack of it has brought down some of the best pro teams in the game.

Remember that nothing will be handed to you. You have to go out and make your own luck. This doesn't mean that you have to find your way onto a pro team to get noticed, but what you have to do is play against the pros and beat the pros. And you want to beat the pros on LAN, which means being able to travel to tournaments. That's how you make a name for yourself and create opportunities. Think of it like a ladder and take it one rung at a time.

Remember that there are very few people who can make it as a pro player, but if you work hard and put in the time, good things will happen. I promise!

stantly playing with the best out there, and playing well against the best, I was able to build my reputation, so when an opportunity presented itself, I could take advantage of it. This got me onto Fear and in the door. I was now on my first pro team, so I just continued to play on the ladders and moved my way up. I then played with EnVyUs, where I was able to learn from a great player named StaiNViLLe before landing on a team called Obey.

Playing with StaiNViLLe was really significant in my development as a player. I went through a lot of team changes and saw the highs and lows of being a pro player. It was all very stressful, but after this I quickly realized that it was all business. It was more than just a game. Money and my reputation were on the line. I was no longer playing a video game for fun. Everybody was trying to win, so I had to put myself in the best possible situation to win as well or else I wouldn't be able to compete consistently at that level. It was a long buildup, but once it did happen, it just exploded.

I had been on Obey for a couple of months when I had the opportunity to attend my first-ever MLG LAN tournament in Dallas 2011. We were like the fifth- or sixth-best team in the game. This was the best team I'd ever been on, but I still wanted more. I knew that I had that potential to be the best even back then, which is why I was so stubborn. I just didn't think that I had the players around me to win, and if you're not winning, it's really hard to call yourself the best.

My more immediate concern was my mom. She almost didn't let me go at all until she learned that we had a sponsor in place who would pay for the flight and hotel room. That eased her mind a little bit, but she was still worried. I was young and would be traveling there on my own, so she was freaking out and concerned that somebody was going to do something to me. "What if these people are just paying for you to go so they can hurt you?" I tried everything. I showed her YouTube videos and live streams, but I could tell that she was not on board. That's when I knew that I needed to win this tournament and show her that I could bring home a substantial amount of prize money or she might not let me do something like this ever again. In order to do that, I needed to be on a better team. Placing fifth or sixth just wasn't going to cut it.

A week before the tournament, I told my teammates on Obey that I didn't want to be on the team anymore. I was under contract and was begging them to drop me so the contract would be void and I could go to another team. What I was doing was a pretty big deal because if one of your teammates says this before an event, you're not going to sit there next to them and play well. The chemistry will be ruined before you even start the game. After I told them, I took a nap and woke up to a text saying that I had been dropped. I was stoked. I immediately told my mom, but she was so incredibly mad at me. "How could you do this? Use your head!" Even at the time a part of me knew it was stupid, but I also knew that this was the only way I could get this whole thing to work out for me. It's actually funny now. Me and some of those other players look back at it and laugh, but it was a pretty bad move on my part at the time. For those out there looking to be pros, don't do something like this.

Even if I wasn't able to land on another team before Dallas, I was confident that I'd find a new team after the tournament because there were always major team changes after these events. Now this is where I got lucky. Out of the blue, two or three days later, I got a call from Bobby, who now played for a team called Leverage. They had always been a good team and were known as one of the best during *Modern Warfare 2,* so going into *Black Ops 1* they had pretty high hopes. I didn't realize it, but something had happened with his team while my ordeal happened with Obey and now they were looking for a fourth player. He asked me if I could get on a flight to Dallas and be the fourth they needed. This would be the best team I'd been on by far. I had to go to this tournament.

What was great about this was that my mom was really good friends with Bobby's mom. They had met and hung out when we played in local tournaments years earlier. Now she finally felt comfortable with me going because Bobby and his mom would be there. She relaxed and loosened up. I joined Bobby, TeePee, and Aches on

Leverage and we spent the next couple days preparing for MLG Dallas. I had no idea who TeePee and Aches were, and I was always shy in high school, so meeting two new people like this was difficult for me. This was especially true with pro players because I wanted to impress them and prove that I belonged there. It's funny how this all worked out because I've since become really good friends with both. I went to TeePee's wedding last year.

Going into Dallas, I still felt that I needed to win. Even on the plane ride there I was hyping myself up and putting so much pressure on myself because I firmly believed that if I didn't do well I'd never get another opportunity like this again. I didn't even know what these tournaments were like, but I didn't care because I was so dedicated to becoming a professional player. I just loved competing and playing so much. That weekend could have turned out to be the weirdest thing ever and I wouldn't have cared. My mom had been all paranoid that creepy people were going to try to do something to me, but that wasn't the case at all. Everyone there was super cool and super relaxed.

You never really understand the magnitude of how big an event like this is until you are there and see it for yourself. Up to this point, the only thing I knew about these tournaments was what I had seen online. Those little local tournaments I used to play in were nothing like my first-ever MLG event. Back in 2011, there weren't the thousands of fans like there are today, so it was easy for me to make that transition. It felt natural, and we ended up winning the entire tournament after beating Resistance in the finals.

I didn't buy anything with the $2,500 I won. I was always worried that this gaming thing could go south at any time, so I saved all the money I made playing during high school. I was really good about that. More significant than the money was that I proved my mom wrong. Nothing happened to me. I wasn't attacked. Nobody did things to me. Everyone was super cool. I loved being able to throw that in her face. She's always been my best friend and I mess around with her like I would with one of my friends from high school. That's just how our relationship worked.

Over the course of 2011, we began a pretty heated rivalry with OpTic. We were the two best teams and the ones everybody wanted to see play against each other. I knew of OpTic as a sniping team, but as soon as they started a competitive team, every player wanted to join. It was the prestige associated with their name. They were put on a higher level than the other teams. They were starting to take the place of Fear and EnVy, which were the most recognizable teams back in *Call of Duty 2*.

OpTic offered players so many other opportunities to further their careers. If you wanted to start doing YouTube, you'd have an instant following because you were on OpTic Gaming. They mixed personality with competitiveness and they did it right. At Leverage, we didn't have that. We were strictly win, win, win, and don't worry about anything else but winning. I hadn't done YouTube yet myself, but it was appealing to me for sure. I thought it would be cool to be able to post game play and get your name out there on YouTube. It was like another challenge for me.

I wanted to join OpTic, but I was under contract with Leverage. This was all eerily similar to what I had just experienced with Obey, and after the way my mom reacted to how I handled that situation, I couldn't do the same thing again. I had to do it the right way, but the problem was that the owner of Leverage wouldn't let me out of this contract. I guess he didn't want me to leave because he saw me going to OpTic as me going to the competition. This transition would have to be much more professional, but for the rest of this *Black Ops 1* season, I was stuck and had to ride out the contract.

11

FROM *GTA* TO *COD*

MiDNiTE

Ah, man, Scumpii kind of stole my theme. I was going to talk about timing and luck because that's exactly what happened to me. I never played competitively, so my path to joining OpTic was completely different, but I was lucky to have things work out the way they did. It was really more like fate. It all happened so quickly. I happened to know this girl who I met through another girl who I met through another girl. I definitely worked hard, but I also got a little lucky. That's why it was really important to me that I kept working hard and let my videos do my talking.

When I was playing *Call of Duty* online in 2009, I'd play constantly, but I didn't have any friends on Xbox. The scene was all guys, but one time I was playing a free-for-all when I stumbled upon another girl for the first time ever. Her name was Missstress. I was shocked because I had never met a girl gamer on the Internet before. It felt like I'd just found a unicorn. It was so cool, but I also had to scratch this competitive itch because I wanted to beat her. We started talking and became pals. Anna—that was her real name—had all these other girl gamer friends and she invited me to play *Call of Duty* with them. Their clan was called DM8X and it was the first clan I was a part of. I wasn't even sure what this meant since it was all so new to me, but I was excited to be a part of it.

In December 2009, the girls showed me this sniper montage created by a guy named OpTic H3CZ. I was blown away and immediately started looking up all the other OpTic videos. These guys were doing these crazy things with these weapons that not everyone used. Even the intro with their logo stood out to me. They created it specifically for their videos. I had never seen anything like this before. *Wow, this guy is doing exactly what I want to do.* I used to love making videos when I was a kid. Even in school I had taken a few video production classes. The classes were all centered around school news, which I found to be boring, but the bare-bones part of it, like filming, editing, and putting it together to form a final product, was interesting to me.

The other girls started telling me, "You should make videos. You should buy a capture card because you're really good." I already had a laptop, so I was halfway there. My friend then sent me an Amazon link for an EzCAP 2.0, which is this horrible capture card that cost like ten dollars. You could use this with a standard-issue TV as long as you had all the other cables hooked up. The first video I uploaded was literally just a scoreboard of me getting twenty kills in a Search and Destroy game. I liked the way that I could show people what I was doing, so I got more into it. I started to pay more attention to the sniper videos people like Hutch were making. He was talking about the OpTic clan and I was thinking, *That's so cool.* They were a group of like-minded people who were all doing this stuff that I wanted to do. Then I found other videos where people did these commentaries. They were just talking about whatever they wanted over this *Call of Duty* game play.

Even though there weren't any other girls out there doing this kind of stuff, I knew that I could do it. That's what fueled my fire. I wanted to see what kind of videos I could make. With video making, it always felt like I was sharing a memory or a small story with someone. That's what drove me to make videos. This was long before I knew it was possible to make money off of YouTube. It was more like a hobby that I thought was really fun. If you have passion for something, you can do it all day long and it will never get boring.

I was known as one of the try-hards who was always using the best guns and the best perks in order to get the best score. After watching that H3CZ video, I wanted to learn how to snipe and make a montage. Some of the girls in the clan helped me get started and then I sniped for like an entire month straight in every game I played. I didn't use any other weapons besides the Intervention and the Barrett. I would do 1v1s with my friends just to learn how to make these cool videos that all these other guys were making. I was dedicated and it became a passion. It sounds weird to have a passion for using a certain weapon in a certain video game for a certain purpose, but I was addicted to it. I needed to get better and I think that's what drew people to *Call of Duty*. It's that addiction that made me want to be better than the other people I was playing against. That was the challenge for me.

One of the other girls in the clan was QSL, which stood for "Quick Scoping Lauren," and she was this crazy sniper girl who had already gotten into OpTic. In May 2010, she reached out to me because she was recruiting players for an OpTic girls' team that H3CZ wanted to put together. She told me, "You make good videos and you're a strong player." I had a Skype call with Di3seL, H3CZ, OpTicJ, MerK, and a few of the others. They put all of us girls in the lobby to make sure that we could actually play the game. They liked what I was doing and welcomed me aboard. It was absolutely unbelievable. This YouTube team who I was watching a few months ago just invited me to join. I was ecstatic!

My passion for making videos can be traced back to when I was a kid. My dad loved to make home movies. Our living room was filled with a bunch of these VHS tapes that showed us doing things like going to the park and feeding the ducks. I always thought that was really cool, so I'd reuse the tapes to film stuff like me doing tricks on the trampoline. I loved to make my own music videos and these horrible horror movies with my cousins. I probably recorded over a ton of family memories. Even when I was young, the part I enjoyed the

H3CZ ON
THE OPTIC GIRLS' TEAM

While we were making the move into eSports, I also had my eye on another emerging market at the time. Girl gamers had their own clans and following on YouTube, but we decided to take that one step further by creating a separate OpTic girls' team. I felt this would be a great new way to diversify the brand while attracting more fans in the process. So I did what any man in my position would. We went after the best talent to represent OpTic. Di3seL gave me a list of girls who were playing video games and creating video content. We held tryouts and we formed a team. I also felt it was important that we didn't segregate by having them only post to a girls' channel, so they posted to the main OpTic Nation channel as well.

Unfortunately, our gaming subculture took a little bit longer to welcome women into the space. We received a lot of flak from fans who thought that there were other players out there more deserving to be members of OpTic. The consensus among this group was that the only reason these girls were on OpTic was because they were girls. That was true in a way. Obviously that's why some fans tuned in to watch their content, but they were also entertainers who brought something different to the brand and the scene. In a way, those doubters did have a point because the OpTic girls' team didn't pan out as I originally envisioned. We only ended up keeping two members. One was named Jewel and she was amazing at the game. The second was a little more unique. Ashley Glassel, or OpTic MiDNiTE as she soon became known, was a born YouTuber.

What made MiDNiTE stand out was that she was really good on the micro-phone. Her personality shined and she was already making professional-style videos. She knew how to talk to the camera and relay her story. Fans related to her. To me, that talent was invaluable. The ideas she came up with also stood out because she wasn't doing what all the other girls were doing. She wasn't trying to manipulate sexuality to get viewers. She was actually all about the game. She was already great at commentating, but once she learned how to open up a little more to the audience, things started to click for her.

Ashley was the breakthrough artist of sorts who made me look at the game from a different perspective. It wasn't until she came on board that I realized YouTube wasn't only for *Call of Duty* or for men. She was playing different games. It opened up the catalog for me to see OpTic from a three-dimensional perspective.

most was trying to edit everything together so it looked like an actual movie.

Growing up just outside of the Twin Cities in the nineties, I loved spending time outdoors doing stuff like camping and fishing, but gaming has been a part of my life ever since I was five years old. My dad brought home an NES and I got hooked early on *Madden*. Whenever we'd go to Blockbuster, I'd always try to rent the new *Madden* so I could take the Vikings to the Super Bowl, since, and let's face it, the Vikings weren't going to make the Super Bowl in real life. We'd go to Blockbuster because the games were pretty expensive to buy. I'd only buy a game if I knew I would be playing it constantly.

Things were good until seventh grade when my parents sat me and my sister down in the living room to tell us they were getting a divorce. I couldn't believe this was actually happening to my family. Immediately I just started crying. My dad stayed living in our house while my mom got an apartment. My younger sister, Sydney, and I basically lived out of a suitcase as we were shuffled back and forth between parents. Every week I'd box up my PlayStation 2 to bring over to my mom's place. I used to hate Sundays because that was the transition day when we had to pack. This whole period in my life was awful, but it did bring me and my sister closer. We played a lot of video games together—well, I would play and she would watch because I wasn't into sharing. I kinda feel bad about that now because I just wouldn't let her play.

This was hard on me, but it was really hard on my dad. He turned to alcohol to cope and I just had to sit back and watch him change into a completely different person right before my eyes. We didn't do anything together anymore, and I couldn't talk to him. I had nobody to confide in. I didn't have very many close friends, and even if I did, I couldn't tell them what was going on, so I spent most of my time alone in my room with my PlayStation 2. I would lock my door and completely lose myself in games like *Grand Theft Auto*. I started playing *GTA* back in 1997. It was the overhead bird's-eye-view version. It's a really simple game, but I just loved how you could literally do whatever you wanted in that game. This was one of the few games I made sure to buy because I'd play it all the time. Instead of going to the mall or hanging out with other kids, I would stay home and play *GTA*.

Middle school was tough. Things at home weren't good, and to top it off I was really confused about my sexuality. One day when I was in eighth grade I was riding the bus home when this kid started calling me a lesbian. I had no idea what that even meant, but eventually I figured it out from television of all things. The worst part was that I didn't even know if that was me or not. I didn't know what I felt because I had been attracted to girls and guys. I didn't really begin to feel comfortable in my own skin until I was a junior in high school. I met a whole bunch of really cool people through the Gay-Straight Alliance and it was also when I met my first-ever girlfriend, Amanda. That relationship didn't work out and it made senior year really difficult for me, but I managed to pull through and graduate even though it didn't look like that was going to happen. No matter what I was going through, video games were the way I'd cope. Sometimes it felt like that was the only thing I enjoyed doing.

Things got so much better between me and my dad when I graduated, but he also put a lot of pressure on me to either go to college

GAMER TAG TALES

When I first met Missstress, my gamer tag was Awesome-O, like the robot from *South Park*. I thought that was hilarious. Then I became obsessed with the show *The Office*. I thought everything about Michael Scott was funny—particularly the screenplay he wrote called *Threat Level Midnight*. I couldn't fit that whole title into a fifteen-character gamer tag, so I cut it down to thrtlvlmidnight. It was kind of lame and nobody could tell what it was. OpTicJ used to call me Turtle Midnight because that's what it looked like to him. I never picked "Midnight," but that's what the girls I was playing with at the time would always call me. I thought my other gamer tag was ugly, so I wanted to just change it to Midnight, but I couldn't get any variation of Midnight that wasn't taken until I got into OpTic. That's when I had the opportunity to get a cool-looking name, so I went with OpTic MiDNiTE. Hector really liked it as well, and we had this guy who drew up graphics for my YouTube channel make it look all space-themed. I've stuck with it ever since then.

or learn a trade. I knew he was right, but it still led to a ton of arguments. I enrolled in a local community college near my house and I took a couple courses, but immediately I knew that this was not what I should be doing. It wasn't that I was lazy or didn't want to work hard, but I just knew that this wasn't a good fit. I stopped going after one semester. I decided to give school one more shot and enrolled at Dakota Technical College, but after two semesters there, I had that same feeling again. I didn't have any passion for what I was studying. There were things that I would much rather be learning about. I always wanted to go to film school, but I just wasn't in a financial position to pursue that.

In February of 2008, I said screw it and decided to find a full-time job. My mother helped me land a position at Costco since she worked for the company. My job was to scan people's cards to see if they were spending enough money to qualify for an upgraded membership program. I'd always hang around the checkout line, so I spent a lot of time talking to this guy named Dimas and some of the other cashiers who I worked with. We were both into games and we'd pretty much talk about that all day. He asked, "Have you ever played *Call of Duty 4*? It's selling like crazy." He explained to me how it was a first-person shooter, but I didn't play those. "I'm more of a *Grand Theft Auto* kind of girl," I told him.

I was curious, so I bought the game and played through the entire campaign in one sitting. For five or six hours I didn't even move. I was just so enthralled. It was like this modern war story was playing out like a movie in front of me. I was hooked. The next day at work, I told Dimas how I beat all the levels. "Levels? Did you play multiplayer?" I saw the option on the screen, but it didn't register with me that multiplayer was the reason why people bought the game. "What's multiplayer?" He told me all about it, so I went home that night and played multiplayer. It quickly became an addiction. I just thought it was so cool and I needed to play more because the people I was playing against online were just so much better than me.

MIDNITE'S FAVORITE GAME GROWING UP

This is an easy one. *Grand Theft Auto: San Andreas* came out when I was in tenth grade and I played it constantly. This was already my favorite franchise at the time, but they added so many cool and crazy things that I was just like, holy crap! The game had that addiction factor. There wasn't a game that caught my interest the way this did until I started playing *Modern Warfare 2* a few years later.

PART 3

MODERN
WARFARE 3

12

CALL OF DUTY EXPERIENCE

OpTicJ

Right smack-dab in the middle of the *Black Ops 1* competitive season, Activision hosted the first-ever *Call of Duty* Experience (or *Call of Duty* XP as it's known) in September 2011. This was a massive multimedia spectacle-type event to promote the release of their brand-new game, *Modern Warfare 3*. At the center of it all was a million-dollar eSports tournament where the winning team would take home $400,000. Yes, $400,000. This was by far the biggest prize pool ever in the history of *Call of Duty* eSports.

Nothing even came close to what was going on that weekend. They definitely got the experience part right. It wasn't just a tournament. It was a spectacle. The event was held in an old airplane hangar in Los Angeles that had been used as a movie sound stage in the past. The place was huge. Outside there were all of these *Call of Duty*–related activities. There was a paintball course and a zip line. You could go off-roading in these *Call of Duty*–style jeeps that took you through this military reenactment that was made to resemble a mission with real soldiers. They even set up a real-life Burger Town, which was the food stand just like the fictional restaurant from the game. After the tournament, Kanye West was going to perform. It was all pretty amazing.

This was a dream come true for a gaming culture that was already hyper in love with *Call of Duty*. The entire environment was electric. There were a lot of industry people there, and a bunch of others who had made a living off *Call of Duty* videos. I was meeting all of these people that I had only met online, and then running into others who I had seen only briefly at some events. For the first time ever, the entire *Call of Duty* community was united physically all in one place. It just felt like the embodiment of a multiplayer experience playing out in real life right before our eyes.

THE KILL FEED AT COD XP

Not only was I representing my friends at OpTic during the event, but I was the cohost of a show on Machinima called *The Kill Feed.* We filmed an episode on location at the event. You can find it online if you want to reminisce. For those of you who never saw it, *The Kill Feed* was a show built around an app that Machinima was releasing on Facebook called the Respawn Army. This was our attempt to take what worked with the hard-core gaming audience on YouTube and see if it worked on Facebook. This was an app native to Facebook that would help discover new talent, feature existing talent, and find an interactive way for the social gamers and hard-core gamers to interact with each other. The show was an attempt to curate that audience.

Set up throughout the hangar were all of these stations where you could play *Modern Warfare 3* for the first time. The game wasn't scheduled to be released for another two weeks. Nobody had seen it before, not even the players who were about to compete in the tournament. This was exciting, but there was also some anxious anticipation. The strategies and map recognition that had helped teams be effective in the previous *Black Ops 1* season wouldn't be the same in this tournament. Everybody was playing off of pure speculation. Without anyone knowing the game, it would end up being a free-for-all, so all the players had to rely heavily on their teammates. That chemistry had to be really strong coming in.

There were also going to be new game types included in the XP tournament matches that they probably shouldn't have been playing—like Team Deathmatch. This would make for slower game play. From a competitive standpoint, I would look at *CoD* XP as being more like necessary growing pains when it came to the progression of the sport. I wouldn't say it was negative in any way—it was more putting the cart before the horse, if anything. You had Activision, which was a world-renowned publisher of some of the best games on the planet, tapping into eSports in a very serious manner. They were thinking through how that all worked and still learning the territory. This was a very early and raw version of eSports that hadn't been tweaked for optimal viewership yet, but any aspect that was lacking from a competitive standpoint was overshadowed by the stage the game was now being played on.

When it came time for the tournament to be played, they removed all the seats from the hangar. Everyone was just standing in this huge open space and it was jacked full of people. I was surrounded by longtime fans of OpTic. The community really came out to support us (we love all you guys, you're the best). Everyone there was just focused on the main stage. You had the announcers up there. Monitors filled the stage. The floor was a rowdy mess. There was trash everywhere. I was stepping on empty bottles. It was rugged— like being in the middle of a mosh pit. When the matches started, the place erupted. It was a mess, but it was a beautiful mess. eSports was starting to get serious.

This was such a drastic contrast to anything I ever experienced as a player. As I watched how the game and the scene progressed, a part of me wished I had tried to make a run at being a professional player.

At heart, I would have loved to be a professional player of any kind, whether it be soccer or basketball, but especially gaming because that was the one thing I had the most passion for. That addiction was there at the very beginning and it only got more intense when I learned that I could play video games competitively. I was always better than my friends, but when I played in that first LAN tournament in 2007, it was like: *Whoa, hang on a second, these guys are pretty darn good too.* This was a whole different world.

To be a professional, you have to constantly play against people who will challenge you, teach you, and coach you. If you don't have access to that, you're gonna struggle. It's impossible to predict if it would have been possible for me to make it. I had graduated college and was working full-time, but take that out of the equation and I'd like to think that I could have gotten pretty darn close. I might not have, but I like to think it. I can see myself being able to make a short run as a professional, but if I'm being honest with everyone, my peak would probably be as a good amateur. I would be that guy who might get called up, and sure, I could have blown up if I found the right fit with the right team and the chemistry was there, but these teams are so fickle with their roster changes. There are so many different variables that play a factor in what makes a professional career take off. It was a bummer that I couldn't play in something like this, but I knew my talent lay elsewhere.

What I was starting to realize at this point was that I was much better suited at managing these players and helping them make a living than I was trying to actually be one of them. That didn't necessarily mean coaching these guys to be better eSports players, but helping them build a media presence on YouTube. I was also a contributing member of OpTic, so I was posting a game-play video here and there on my own OpTicJ channel. I was loosely involved in deals if H3CZ needed an extra set of eyes or help consulting. It was all done for free and in the best interest of this team that I've been a part of for the past five years.

I was also one of the original members making some of the early

OH REALLY!

The career of OpTicJ could have been very, very different. J could have actually been one of the early pioneers of vlog-style videos. Back in 2010, he came up with this series called *Oh Really,* which was one of the very first day-in-the-life-style video series we ever did. It was probably the first time anyone in the community did something like this. It was all about going behind the scenes to see what we do at events and it was all shot like a documentary. We did this at our very first tournament in Dallas. It got a lot of views, but with the growing responsibility he had at Machinima and the fact that it would cost us extra money to take him on the road, it was difficult for us to commit to the series. We were so heavily focused on making OpTic work that the budget was tight. He's really done so many different things for us and has worn so many different hats. His role has changed over the years, so some of the newer fans might not know about his early contributions that helped grow OpTic.

—H3CZ

decisions about the direction of the eSports team. What's funny was that when we started the team a year earlier, in 2010, we didn't really expect much. It was an experiment. We actually joked around because we always thought that it would only be a small part of the company. Now here we were playing for the chance to take home a $400,000 grand prize.

When it came to eSports, OpTic wasn't considered a contender right away. We had only won one LAN event prior to XP. We were never that dominant *Call of Duty* team who won championship after championship. We did find significant success by being the most recognizable *Call of Duty* team with one of the biggest gaming channels on YouTube. Because of that, the outpouring of support from our fans was there. They've always backed us up from day one and without them none of this would have ever been possible. Whether we placed first or not, the fans were always there showing their support.

In a weird kind of way, this actually played in our favor during *CoD* XP because we were looked at as the underdog who also had the ability to win. It was like your typical Disney sports movie where this group of guys who have all this potential go out and get crushed the first time they step onto the field. They then band together and rally to defeat the villains and earn this major victory. Maybe it's not exactly the same, but you get the gist. This didn't mean that we didn't care about winning. If anything, the opposite was true. We didn't want to have a failing eSports division, so there was increased pressure on us to put winners in OpTic jerseys.

13

RAGS TO RICHES

BigTymeR

ake up, bitch! Welcome back to another chapter! I know, that intro doesn't work as well on paper. I've actually been trying to get away from the intro lately. A few years down the road when I try to get a job, I'll have hundreds of YouTube videos out there of me yelling "Wake up, bitch!" That probably doesn't look great.

But right now I'm here and ready to bang out the next installment, so I hope you're ready to get your learn on. We're talking *CoD* XP today. What I'm gonna do to help enhance your experience is provide you with a little playlist. On the next page is a little taste of what I was listening to at the time so you guys can play along at home.

Anyway, the million-dollar tournament! That's kind of deceiving. It's not like anybody won a million dollars. The first-place team took home $400,000, which meant that each player got $100,000, but it was really only $76,000 after taxes. Either way, people started freaking the fuck out when they announced the size of that prize pool. Everyone was super fired up, but that quickly ended when we learned that we had to play a game that nobody had ever seen before. Awesome. That

BIG T'S PLAYLIST FOR THE COD XP CHAPTER

The first one on this list is "Donald Trump," and I was only listening to this at XP because there was a verse in the song where he says something about making a hundred grand, which was exactly how much money we were each playing for. So I just played that song on repeat and it made me feel like Mac Miller trying to make that money. We're gonna round out the playlist with QuESt and Meek Mill. I went on to listen to "Dreams and Nightmares" before every match during *Black Ops 2*. Not for any particular reason. I just loved the song. I was a big fan of rap music because a lot of the stories being told were about working hard and taking big risks in life in order to fulfill your dreams, which was similar to what we were doing. Granted, we weren't gangbanging and rapping, but we did put our lives on hold to take this extreme risk. That's why I relate to rap.

1. Mac Miller, "Donald Trump"
2. QuESt, "Hunger"
3. Meek Mill, "Dreams and Nightmares"

kind of took the wind out of our sails, but this was still a huge tournament. It put OpTic on the eSports map. This is also what convinced my parents to let me do this full-time, so it does hold a pretty special place in my heart. With that money I got an apartment, bought some furniture, and then got my mom a Honda Accord. I put the rest in the bank and, a couple years later, would turn it into $900,000. More on that later.

In spite of all the many ways we each benefited, looking back now, *CoD* XP wasn't the most competitive tournament. If we're being brutally honest, that whole tournament was kind of a giant clusterfuck. And I mean that in the nicest way possible. It's just that I don't think they cared much about competitive game play or the players. The entire event was *Call of Duty* XP, but the tournament was only a small part of it. The point was to showcase the game and throw a million dollars out there to hype it up.

There were so many other events and activities going on outside, but we didn't get to do shit. I know that I really wanted to try the zip line. I was kind of bummed we couldn't, but we literally didn't have any time. The entire weekend was spent preparing for the matches, talking to the staff, or just trying to figure out the schedule. We didn't have a lot of time to "experience" that other stuff. This was big money for us, so we were there focused. All work and no play.

That team we put together for *CoD* XP kind of came out of nowhere. This was right in the middle of the *Black Ops 1* season, so I had settled in playing with MerK, JKap, and Rambo. We were doing well. We'd just won at Columbus a few months earlier. Now, right before the registration, we learned that JKap, who was seventeen, was too young and that Rambo couldn't play either because he came from the only province in Canada that had this gambling restriction that made him ineligible. To this day, they're still pissed at not being able to play in the tournament. I don't think we'll ever hear the end of it from them. That kind of thing still happens a lot today, and there are people who get screwed over every year because you have to be eighteen to play in *CoD* Champs, and some of the best *Call of Duty* players out there are only sixteen or seventeen years old. Me and MerK were actually panicking because we didn't know who we were going to play with.

At first we tried to team up with TeePee and ProoFy, but they ended up playing for Leverage. Just a couple days before the roster had to be locked, we picked up NaDeSHoT. He had proven himself when stepping up for Rambo back in Dallas, so that was an easy choice. For our fourth we ended up going with Vengeance, who had played with Matt before, but not with the rest of us. I'm pretty sure I've never had one conversation with him. He was good at the game, but I don't think he called out one time. There was no communication going on, but it wasn't like we knew what to call out in this game since we'd never played it. After *CoD* XP, Vengeance kind of stepped away, but according to his Twitter, he's gone on to be a UFC fighter and looks super jacked in this picture of him online. He mentions *Black Ops 3*, so I guess he still plays. Anyway, it was a weird team, but it obviously worked out for the best.

We still weren't in the tournament yet. We had to qualify. As far as the rules went, this wasn't anything like an MLG-sanctioned tour-

COD XP:
H3CZ'S FAN PERSPECTIVE

When I heard that there was going to be this massive *Call of Duty* event, the first thing that went through my head was that the amount of content I could get out of this would be nuts. It was a YouTuber's playground. They had these prestige tokens or badges that you could earn by completing various events like the off-road jeep rides and the zip line. It was a carnival. It felt like we were living out the game in reality. I also made this GoPro video of me running around the paintball map shooting the crap out of people. They set up the course to resemble the Scrapyard from the game. You can still check it out on my channel.

I took a step back and let the players play. To me, this tournament was about being a fan. I was excited to play *Modern Warfare 3* just like everyone else who was there, but my favorite thing about this tournament (other than OpTic taking first place) was the fact that I got to meet all of my online friends in person for the very first time. There were all these people there that I had made videos with and collaborated with who I never got to meet before. This was the first time I ever got to meet Hutch in person. OpTic had been traveling with the competitive team, but that was much different. This event wasn't just for the eSports players. All the YouTubers were out in full force and that is what made this such an amazing event.

nament. Even the qualification was strange. There were all these different registrations on the website that got folks all confused. Then we had to play public matches on *Black Ops 1,* but we ended up being one of the thirty-two teams selected into the tournament, and there wasn't a losers' bracket. It was one and done. We just played best of fives. That's why we were so nervous going into each match because we knew that if we lost we were out.

The bracket played a huge role and there was a lot of controversy going into it. The way they did it was to pull names out of a hat. The first two teams they pulled out would play each other and so on. The problem was that they only had thirty-one pieces of paper in the hat and none of those pieces had our team name on it. People were thinking that we planned that, or that we took our name out to ensure we got an easier bracket, but that wasn't true. In fact, we were put in a hard bracket anyway, so I don't know why people thought that.

This confusion carried over into the game. All we got were ten minutes to warm up on this game we'd never played. We were jumping in blind and had no idea what we'd were doing. We were so used to being able to come into a tournament knowing exactly what we needed to win a game, but now we were getting thrown onto a map and game mode we'd never played before and forced to use weapons we never used. Good fucking luck. Then again, everybody was in the same boat. It was a level playing field, so it was really more about who could pick up the game faster and learn it in basically one day. When it came to the actual rules, a lot of the items people were using would be considered extremely cheap. I remember NaDeSHoT running around and using items on his weapon that would allow him to see people through walls. It was all a little nuts.

We were one of the best teams there, but we also got really lucky. Still to this day I don't know how we pulled this one off. There were a few close games that could have gone either way and those were a deciding factor in the outcome. One game in particular was a Team Deathmatch against Leverage that we won by one kill. The object of the game mode was to see who could pick up the most kills and we won forty-nine to forty-eight on a map called Underground. We were skillful as well, but little moments like that could have swayed the entire tournament. They thankfully worked out in our favor. On this Leverage team were Teepee, ProoFy, Assassin, and Aches. These were some of the guys we tried to partner with at the beginning and I'm glad we didn't. At one time during the match, I looked over and saw Assassin choking halfway through the game because he hadn't racked up a kill yet.

There were only something like eight North American teams and those were the teams we had to look out for. The rest of the teams were all international. We had played some of these guys online a little bit, but it was hard because the connection was usually awful. In spite of the bad connection, we could still beat them and we could just tell by the way they moved around the map that they weren't that good at *Call of Duty*. Those would be easier matches, though some of the European teams were good as well. The team we played in the finals, Infinity, was from England and they were pretty good.

We actually had a chance to play this team back in 2010 during *Modern Warfare 2,* but I kind of screwed it up for everyone. This was back during a GameStop-sponsored online tournament. It was the first time Europe had ever played North America in *Call of Duty* and those guys were talking loads of shit leading up to the tournament. There were two North American teams and two European teams who were invited to go, but it was Infinity who ended up winning the tournament because we got booted during the qualifying round. This is a bit of a digression, but it's pretty funny, so hang in there for a second and run with me on this.

I was playing with NaDeSHoT and Axel (who doesn't play anymore, so you probably never heard of him) and I don't know who the fourth was, but we were playing a match against Team Replay. Whatever was going on that day, my connection back in Arkansas wasn't working. I don't know if there was a tornado or what, but I couldn't get online. I went over to a friend's house to play from there, but that wasn't working either. So, fuck me. What I did was have somebody recover my account and play for me. I can't for the life of me remember who it was that played in my place, but it doesn't matter. It's obviously cheating because you can't do that.

OpTic ended up winning without me, but Replay somehow knew

NADESHOT'S SIDE OF THE STORY

This is one of my absolute favorite stories. All BigTymeR had to do was say nothing. Literally, just say nothing. As long as nobody said anything, we would have been fine. The other team didn't know. They had a clue, but they didn't know and couldn't prove anything. When they accused us of account recovery we just denied, denied, denied so we could still play in this tournament and win this money. And we had a very good chance of winning since we were so much better than the other teams. BigTymeR has always been a real smart guy, but back in the day he was this alpha competitor. So yeah, as you'll find out on the next page, he basically admitted to account recovery. Brilliant. Axel and I were livid.

At the time, BigTymeR would give players online lessons in *Call of Duty,* and they would pay him in Microsoft points. This was like Xbox currency that you could use to buy games and online goods. We still had his account information from when we gave it to our friend to play for him. We hacked into his account and saw that he had ten thousand Microsoft points, which was like hundreds and hundreds of dollars. We decided to fuck with him and just buy the dumbest shit imaginable. We bought his avatar a pet monkey and a whole bunch of random costumes that nobody would ever buy to make him look like a total idiot. It's like the equivalent of buying him the orange and blue suits from *Dumb and Dumber.* I mean, he had a virtual pet monkey. Axel and I were crying laughing while we were doing it. We ended up giving him his account back, and luckily he's a laid-back dude, so he didn't make a big deal about it, but it's still one of my favorite stories to this day.

that it wasn't me playing. It was common to have a ringer back in those days. You could usually tell because one of the players wouldn't talk or claimed their microphone wasn't plugged in. That's probably what happened in this case. After the match, it was Miskell from Replay who messaged me. He started giving me shit and said that if I had played they would have won. That made me so mad because I knew we would have beat them even worse if I had been in the game. Me, being the cocky little fuck that I was, wanted to prove myself. So I sent him a message back: "Fuck you! If I did play we would have beat you even worse." I basically admitted that I cheated. He took that message and sent it to GameBattles to get us disqualified from the whole thing. NaDeSHoT was so pissed, and you heard what he did to me.

I knew NaDeSHoT did it. For the longest time I just hated him for that, but I couldn't get him to admit it until we moved into the OpTic House a few years later. Anyway, my dumb ass got us disqualified from this GameStop tournament and the team who went on to win was Infinity from Great Britain. Fast-forward one year and this was the team who we were about to square off against in the finals at *CoD* XP.

We had never seen Infinity play live since there was no streaming at the time, but we were able to check out some of their old-school montages and game play. We had just heard a little bit about how they played and got to watch them during the tournament. A lot of the guys who played on that team, like XLNC and Gunshy, still play today and ended up being really good *Call of Duty* players. They had some confidence going into that final match, but I'll tap out here and let NaDeSHoT tell you about that.

Thanks for reading. Please leave a like if you enjoyed the chapter.

14

NO BATHROOMS BACKSTAGE

NaDeSHoT

There we were. Me, MerK, BigTymeR, and Vengeance. We're all backstage ready to go play the finals against Infinity and I had to take the biggest shit of my life. No joke. It was awful.

My nerves were so bad that I was forced to hold this in with every ounce of strength in my body. I was sweating and crouching on the ground trying not to think. I'm pretty sure I was on the verge of a panic attack. And the guys working the event wouldn't let me go to the bathroom. They wouldn't let any of the players out of their sight because they needed the show to stay on schedule. I don't know if you've ever been backstage at a live show, but the production security guys don't care. They just need to make sure the show runs on time. And there was a lot going on. It was super production-heavy. They were live-streaming. Nick Swardson was announcing a contest winner. They played a recap of the tournament on the big screen. Kanye West was getting ready to perform onstage immediately after the finals. It all made us feel like a novelty act.

In spite of the distractions, this was the biggest match of my life.

It was the chance to finally get my big win for OpTic and prove that I could do it. Activision was now taking a serious interest in competitive *Call of Duty*, and winning this tournament could make OpTic the premier team. This match was also the difference between $50,000 and $100,000. For anyone who is eighteen years old and working a job for an hourly wage, you know that's a big difference. But there was nothing we could do but sit there and wait. They wouldn't let us warm up . . . or go to the bathroom.

I wasn't even on the team going into *CoD* XP, but I was still planning to go the event just to watch and support the guys. I was eighteen and old enough to qualify age-wise, but there was no way I would be able to play in the actual tournament unless another team picked me up. That didn't look like it was going to happen. Back in September 2011, I wasn't this Kobe Bryant– or LeBron James–type of player in *Call of Duty* who was in high demand. People weren't going out of their way to recruit me, so I was always in the position where I had to negotiate my way onto a team. I was confident in my own ability and people knew that I could consistently play well, but my reputation wasn't that of being the best pro player out there who was going to make a huge difference.

When the rules were announced for XP a few weeks before the tournament, we learned that JKap and Rambo couldn't play. Big-TymeR and MerK were scrambling to pick up two more players and at the last minute they called me. I had filled in for Rambo when he was sick earlier in the year, so they knew I could do it. I was jumping for joy when I got that call. I was working at McDonald's at the time, so learning that I suddenly had a chance to play for that $100,000 first prize was like a jolt to my system. It was another situation where I kind of found my way onto a roster at the last minute, but I was loyal to OpTic, so that paid off. A part of me felt like Rudy. I was that guy who was there waiting on the sidelines when they needed somebody to go in. I never had a problem being that guy. I mean, I wasn't going to say no. Nobody was going to refuse to play in a million-dollar tournament, so I hopped on a plane.

I landed in Los Angeles and was looking out at the runway when it all started to become so much more real. Even still, I couldn't wrap my head around the fact that we were actually playing for that much money. I had never won a major tournament before, so I'd never felt that sense of victory or accomplishment that came with that first-place finish on a big stage. I wasn't going into the tournament expecting to win or anything—I wasn't expecting much at all. I just wasn't one of those guys. Some people view it as pessimism, but I think it's more me being realistic, and I've always considered myself a realistic person. All I could do was play my best and see how things turned out. Even before the tournament started, I was so incredibly nervous. I wasn't sleeping that well at night. There was just so much pressure.

The matches were set to begin on Friday, but on Thursday all the teams went to the Westin Hotel by LAX for a consultation held by the organizers. They had the people from Activision there telling us about the event and all the rules that we had to abide by. This was the first time that any North American team was going to play the international teams, so we were seeing teams from Europe, Australia, South Korea, and South America for the very first time. And everybody thought they were the best. Everyone walking around there was so smug and I was just as guilty.

In that room at the Westin there was this team from Sweden. The players were draped in their country's flag like it was a football match. All of a sudden they started laughing at us. We had no idea what they were saying, but we were a little taken aback. *What's going on with these guys?* The organizers gathered everyone around to announce the draw and determine the bracket. It turned out that we would play Sweden in the very first match. Looking back, I kinda feel a little bad because these poor guys had no clue what was about to happen, but at the time I just wanted to kick their ass. North America dominated *Call of Duty*. Most Europeans didn't stand a chance. It was like an American trying to play soccer in Europe. The next day when it came time for the match, we just straight molly-wopped them. Right there during the very first match of the tournament, we wanted to send a message to everyone else and we did.

Not only was I nervous, but it was physically difficult to get comfortable during the matches because the venue itself was so unusual. This wasn't a normal competitive setup. It wasn't easy to play. They had us sitting on metal trash cans. The monitors were two feet above our heads. The AC was jacked up, and it was so loud that you couldn't hear your teammates. This led to some real nitty-gritty matches where we just had to hope for the best. In the end, I'm sure it was just as difficult for everyone else. This was still 4v4 and teams were doing their best to win the tournament. In that sense, it was still extremely competitive.

Whatever we were doing worked because we kept winning. With every team we beat, we were getting $25,000 richer. It was absolutely mind-blowing to me that I was earning this kind of money just by playing *Call of Duty*. This was also what made this the most intense tournament that I've ever been a part of. Before I could wrap my head around what was happening, we had earned a spot in the finals.

So there I was backstage before the finals against Infinity, doubled over in pain and on the verge of an all-out panic attack, when they finally brought us out. Of course, we didn't just start the match. They had to drag this thing out. Justine was up there with Fwiz and HastrO. They announced the teams. The whole time we're just sitting there, waiting. It felt like they were all just screwing with me. My anxiety was through the roof.

When the game finally started, MerK stepped up right away and helped us get out to a quick lead during Capture the Flag. I don't even know when in the match it happened, but my nerves went away while we played. Toward the end of the match, we struggled a little bit in Kill Confirmed, but came back to take Search and Destroy to win the event and the $400,000 grand prize.

I lost my fucking mind and went crazy onstage with everyone else. This was the most unexplainable sensation and probably the biggest adrenaline rush that I will ever have in my life. It was just unbelievable and any words that I come up with right now won't do it justice. Everything after this was a blur. We stuck around for the Kanye performance, and I completely forgot about having to find a bathroom until we got back to the hotel. Now we were each $100,000 richer.

THE OPTIC JUICE

What happened with this team and NaDeSHoT in particular was meant to be. It was like the stars aligning or the perfect storm. You couldn't write a better story, and if you tried, nobody would believe it. Winning XP opened a lot of doors for OpTic, but the reason those doors were opened was because OpTic was the team that won. If any other team had won, the impact on the community wouldn't have been the same because no other team had our following. Who would they have celebrated with? Luckily we had a platform, so we could share this victory with our fans and show them how cool competitive *Call of Duty* can really be. Not only was it about what OpTic as a team accomplished, but it was a showcase for the entire community. This is what jump-started the growth of the scene and put competitive *Call of Duty* on the map.

—H3CZ

XP was in the middle of the 2011 *Black Ops 1* season, and after the tournament I found myself in the same situation I was in after filling in for Rambo back in Dallas. Once again, I had to step back down. It was hard to relinquish my spot, but there was nothing I could do about it. I didn't have any power. If the players didn't want me on the team, it was that simple.

A lot of people think this pissed me off, or gave me a chip on my shoulder, but it was never really like that. Yes, it was motivating. A part of me wanted to prove to people that I could continue to play and win at this level, but it's not like I wasn't benefiting from being on OpTic. Being able to post videos and allow people to see my content was still incredibly beneficial for me. I wouldn't have been able to do that without OpTic, so I had to take not being able to play on the competitive team with a grain of salt. I was still being treated well. Hector did everything possible to accommodate me—and he let me have OpTic Nation for a while. This didn't mean I was going to lie down either. I still continued to play and did everything possible to earn a spot on the competitive team, but that wouldn't happen for a while.

15

MY FIRST YEAR WITH OPTIC

Scump

It sucked that I was too young to play in the first *CoD* XP for *Modern Warfare 3* because that whole event would have been really cool to see in person. I was still on Leverage at the time and they didn't do very well, but I followed it all closely and watched all the streams from home.

After XP, there were still two tournaments left in the *Black Ops 1* season—MLG Orlando and the National Championship in November 2011. Things on Leverage were beginning to go downhill. As the season progressed, we played worse. We placed fifth in Orlando, and then, at Nationals, which was the last and biggest tournament of the year, we ended up getting our worst placing of the year by finishing sixth. This was the tournament that everyone wanted to win because there was so much more money at stake. We sucked. There was definitely tension on the team. Everybody was mad at each other, so the chemistry was shot. It didn't seem like we would ever be able to get back to that place we were at in the beginning of the season when we were putting in work.

Even though we were playing terrible, the owner of Leverage still wouldn't let me out of my contract, but he did let ProoFy out. ProoFy went and joined OpTic for those last two tournaments. I guess they saw me as the player who anchored their team. I had the red hair. I was young. I was good at the game and he wanted to hold on to me as long as he could, so I had to stick it out for a couple more tournaments.

After the season, I learned that ProoFy wanted out of OpTic. I don't know if it was a chemistry issue for him, or if he just wasn't getting along with the guys on the team or what. I have no idea. I do know that he was looking for something new. I was talking to Rambo and sent him some of ProoFy's texts without realizing that ProoFy hadn't told Rambo he wanted to leave. Rambo was like, "No, I had no idea he was trying to do this. I can't have this on my team. If he doesn't want to be here, we'll pick somebody else up."

Shit hit the fan. OpTic dropped ProoFy because of that, and it was a weird situation since I was good friends with everyone. Don't hate me, man! I didn't realize that showing Rambo those texts would get

HA! YEAH, RIGHT!

Sure he didn't do it on purpose! That wasn't the way I saw it at the time. I saw it as Scump being a young and ambitious kid who went out and manipulated the situation to put himself in the best position to succeed while exposing disloyalty in the process. He wanted to take his rightful place on the throne because he was The King. That is a great story, but in all seriousness, I will give Seth the benefit of the doubt. If he's saying it was a happy accident, I'll believe him. In the end, that probably makes the most sense. I don't think he could have planned something like that out. He couldn't predict how Rambo would react. Even the most well-thought-out plan can fall to pieces when other people are involved.

—H3CZ

ProoFy dropped. He was a little salty for a bit, but we quickly put it behind us. I've played with him on OpTic since, and we went to the Red Bull camp together, so we're really good friends now. The way everything went down was kind of unfortunate. It could be interpreted that I screwed him over, but that wasn't my intention at all.

After what seemed like forever, my contract with Leverage was up! OpTic needed their fourth, so they invited me to join. At the end of 2011 I began playing with Rambo, BigTymeR, and MerK during *Modern Warfare 3*. All of these roster moves were done by the players. The first time I ever spoke to Hector was during a Skype call when we discussed the contract. I hadn't even met him at the MLG events. Things are different now, but back in the day the scene was so much smaller. Now we'd all sit down and talk through any roster change to make sure that we're doing what's best for the team. It was much less formal back in the day.

It wasn't hard for me to transition from Leverage to OpTic. If anything, the switch helped me step up my game. I was the youngest and I learned a lot from everyone else around me. Rambo taught me how to play the game on a smarter level. I always had the raw skill and was pretty intelligent when it came to my decision making in the game, but Rambo showed me the correct way to play. He tutored me, mentored me, and molded me into a much better player. He's always been considered one of the smartest players in *Call of Duty* history, so his insight just helped me out tremendously. Rambo, BigTymeR, and MerK were also veterans who had been winning for so long that it took a lot of the pressure off me. There were a lot of little things I picked up just by watching them play—like seeing how they performed in stressful situations. The more I played with them, the more I learned and the more I grew as a player.

I was stoked to finally be on OpTic, but it was also a bit of a letdown because for some reason we couldn't play *Modern Warfare 3* on LAN. It was kind of like back in the *MW2* days. This ended up being a dead game for *Call of Duty*. Many pros didn't play it—not because it was a bad *Call of Duty*. There wasn't anything off about the game play, but it couldn't run on LAN. That's the most important thing for competitive *Call of Duty*. I don't know what the problem was. I don't know if the people running the LANs didn't see the potential in the game, so they didn't want to host it, or if there was a certain way you had to set it up so you could play. If that was the case, why wouldn't they just ask the European LAN centers how to do it? I have no idea. Maybe the organizers felt that there wouldn't be a lot of competition, so they decided to wait until next year and hit it hard then.

DON'T LISTEN TO HIM—THAT IS NOT THE REASON WHY

The reason why there were no *Modern Warfare 3* LAN tournaments in North America was because the game had no developer support from Infinity Ward. For MLG, the game has to be easy to set up on a large scale. All we really needed were offline lobbies to be created. Whenever you set up a tournament, you need to connect all of the Xboxes without an Internet connection because an Internet connection would screw up everything. It has to be done offline. With *Modern Warfare 3*, there was no way to create a lobby to even get into a game offline. We needed Infinity Ward to code in an offline lobby. I'm sure it's not that simple, but if they cared at all about competitive *Call of Duty*, they would do things like that.

We had been asking for offline lobbies since *Call of Duty 4*. We had contacted the Infinity Ward reps, and every single year they'd give us the same tired lines: "Okay, we'll look into it and see what we can do." Every year they would promise us an offline lobby, but they never came through, which is why most *Call of Duty* players are frustrated with Infinity Ward. It was Treyarch who changed all that with *Black Ops 1* and, later, *Black Ops 2*.

—BigTymeR

Okay, well, there you go. Thanks for making me look like an idiot. The point I'm making is that all of the LAN tournaments for *Modern Warfare 3* were overseas. The problem was that OpTic wouldn't be able to fly a team overseas to compete. The game wasn't that big, so Hector didn't want to deal with all that, but we still figured out a way to play. Hector told us that as long as we didn't sign any contracts, we could find a different team that would pay for our travel. He didn't want to hold us up or prevent us from competing. That's what we did.

In the spring of 2012, MerK, BigTymeR, Rambo, and I joined a team called Apex North America specifically so we could play *Modern Warfare 3* overseas. It was understood that we would all come back to OpTic after. It was basically an interim period, and there was no way to play in the U.S., so Hector never saw it as us betraying him.

There was no more begging my mom to let me go on trips. She was on board and supportive with gaming as long as I kept my grades above a B. If I did my part, she would let me do what I wanted, and I made sure that my grades never dropped because I knew what was at stake. She knew that I wanted to do this, so there was no way she was going to take it away from me without good reason. This was definitely weird because not long before, I wasn't allowed to go to tournaments that were two hours away. Now I was hopping a plane to a completely different country. It was weird how things worked out and how quickly this all changed.

I was the only one on the team still in high school. I was a junior and had to take a bunch of time off from school. Thank God the school was now much cooler with me taking days off than it had been the past couple years. It used to be that my school only allowed a certain number of sick days, so my mom would be freaking out. During *Black Ops 1* with Leverage, it was much more difficult. We ended up finding a loophole in the system so I would be able to go to these events. What I did was fill out these Educational Trip Forms whenever I went to a tournament. So whatever city I was in at the time, I'd go find a museum or some historical sites. I guess it qualified as an educational experience. Thankfully, I didn't have to do that anymore.

I had never been to Europe before and I think this might have been the first time a North American team flew over there to play. This was an eye-opening experience. Luckily, I was with a bunch of older guys who really helped me out. One of the first places we visited was in England, but we didn't get to see much. We were just there to play. It's not like we were in London or any other major city where there was a lot going on. We stayed in this small town called Blackpool and there wasn't much to do there. Even the Europeans would joke around and make fun of it. This was a dull town where very little happened, so we'd just hang out and focus on the tournaments.

IF I HAD TO DO IT OVER AGAIN

In retrospect, I should have just fronted the money and paid for the team to travel to Europe. It was hard to let go of such a good team and let them play for someone else, but I had bigger goals than just a trophy at the time. Not being able to play *MW3* on LAN was tough for all of us in the community. It hurt me and it hurt OpTic. This wasn't an ideal situation, but the players handled it the right way. It's not like they just got up and left. Rambo approached me and told me what they wanted to do, which basically involved me flying the team out to London. I told them that I couldn't do that, so they worked out an arrangement with another team willing to fund their travel. When they decided to come back, I welcomed them with open arms.

—H3CZ

After playing about four or five tournaments overseas, we all came back to rejoin OpTic. We finished out the *MW3* season in the fall of 2012 with a bunch of online tournaments hosted by 360 Icons. They hosted tournaments every weekend. These were a lot like the

2Ks and 5Ks we play now. The Icons tournaments were smaller, but we also played about three or four bigger tournaments like Frag Cup. We had a great year. We won most of the tournaments we played and didn't place out of the top two all year. Personally, I was killing it. *MW3* was my most consistently successful *Call of Duty*. We put in work and it was a grind, but things really got hectic for me when I started my YouTube channel. Between making videos, practicing, and going to school, I'd only sleep three or four hours a night. I was on a really crazy schedule, but it paid off in the long run.

Everyone's YouTube has to start somewhere. When I started my channel, I got really lucky. Literally the first video I posted on my channel got a shout-out from the YouTuber Ronaldinho. I had actually known him for a while. We had done this charity event together, Call of the Community, where YouTubers and pro players would team up to play. There would be two YouTubers and two pro players on each team. That's when I got to know him and a lot of other YouTubers like TmarTn. I hadn't had a chance to meet any of these guys before, so it was a pretty sweet experience. It helped me out because the hardest part about being a YouTuber is getting started. You typically don't get any views and have to build up your subscribers, but after this shout-out I had five thousand new subscribers overnight. This gave me a pretty big base to start growing my channel.

Now I had to come up with actual ideas for the videos. I think I speak for a lot of successful YouTubers when I say that is the biggest challenge there is. How can I be innovative and come up with something that hasn't been done before? I didn't have a whole lot of time to figure this out because things were about to get positively insane with the release of *Black Ops 2* in November 2012. I wouldn't let this opportunity slip through my fingers, so I dedicated myself to pumping out as much content as I possibly could.

PART 4

BLACK OPS 2

16

ONE STEP BACK AND TWO STEPS FORWARD

Fwiz

OpTic helped make me the biggest commentator in *Call of Duty*, but I got so much shit for it too. This was a double-edged sword. Was it ever an issue that I was commentating OpTic matches while a member of OpTic? All the time! Did people ever bring up a conflict of interest? At every single event!

People were always like "Go figure, he picked OpTic." "He's so biased toward OpTic." "He only gets excited when OpTic does something great." I've heard it all, but I've always been mindful of it and tried my best to stay balanced. In spite of my efforts, it was obvious that I got much more excited when OpTic was doing well. I didn't know how to change that, but I like to think I did a really good job of predicting when OpTic would lose. I wasn't delusional and picking OpTic every match because they were my team. I was biased when it came to that, but I loved commentating OpTic and tried to schedule their matches whenever I could.

The best experience I've ever had commentating OpTic was at

CoD XP in 2011. It was also the biggest crowd I ever commentated in front of. There were tens of thousands of people. The whole thing was wild! Nobody knew what to expect. OpTic had a different roster. The players hadn't even seen *Modern Warfare 3* yet, which made it difficult to play, but it also made it difficult to commentate. I got to play the game a little bit before the event to help feel out some of the maps. The players couldn't play it at all because the organizers didn't want to give anybody a competitive advantage. Even with that very basic knowledge, it was still really tough for me. I could talk about the play styles, but I didn't know the guns they were using. I knew the modes, but not how the modes played on the maps. Still, I had much more sympathy for the players. They were playing in a million-dollar tournament with a lot on the line, whereas I knew I was getting a check and could rely on some improvised humor to get through it.

Just when it looked like everything was about to take off, *Modern Warfare 3* pulled the scene back two years by not having LAN tournaments. This was all reminiscent of *Modern Warfare 2,* only this time we had a taste of what *Call of Duty* could become after *Black Ops 1*. It felt like we were finally on our way up. The thing that was so strange about all this was that MW3 was one of my most financially lucrative games for a commentator, but I only had two jobs. *CoD* XP was the first, and the second was this series called *Friday Night Fights,* which was produced for an online service created by Activision called *Call of Duty* Elite.

I took two weeks off from work to shoot this show. Each episode followed two teams prepping and then playing a match that HastrO and I commentated. The series was filmed on the Sony Pictures studios lot. It was a big deal at the time, but it wasn't traditional eSports. The rules were the same and the games were 4v4, but other than a few gamers and YouTubers, the show was really more about featuring the athletes and Hollywood stars who were also competing in this tournament-style show. Rampage Jackson played. Michelle Rodriguez was in an episode. The goal was to show this wide range of people who played the game.

It was kind of counterproductive to what we were trying to do with eSports. It didn't make fun of the sport by any means, but it wasn't legitimate either. This show wasn't serious. There was competition, but it wasn't eSports. There is kind of an elitist mentality in eSports, so this show was frowned upon by the die-hard community, who viewed it more as a shoot-the-television kind of show. I think it left a sour taste in everyone's mouth because there wasn't anything else happening in eSports at the time. I thought it was pretty neat and I was grateful to be able to do it. I was now making more money than I ever had before, but it also felt like I was in limbo during *Modern Warfare 3* because I wasn't casting any big events.

OH YEAH, I REMEMBER FRIDAY NIGHT FIGHTS

OpTic played on one episode of that, and it was a really cool experience, but it was strange. Stacy Keibler hosted the show, which was awesome. I guess she was dating George Clooney at the time, so he showed up on the set one day. The whole thing was really weird because the show wasn't scripted, but we had to forcefully talk shit to each other. We weren't being serious, so it was all completely fake. We didn't know what the hell to do, so I don't think we really pulled that off. I still have people tweet me after they find that video and ask, "What the fuck is this? What am I watching right now?"

—BigTymeR

Now that I was working full-time at Machinima, my contribution to OpTic was minimal. I compare it to a hip-hop group who record together, but also have their own individual solo projects that end up elevating the group as a collective entity. If I grew as a personality, then I was also helping OpTic grow. I was still making fun videos and

FWIZ'S OWN PERSONAL OPTIC HALL OF FAME TEAM

If I were making my own competitive dream team, and had every player who ever put on an OpTic jersey to choose from, I would anchor it with the two most famous duos in OpTic's competitive history. BigTymeR and Rambo were great together for so many years, and as you are about to find out if you didn't know already, so were NaDeSHoT and Scump. They changed the face of the game. FormaL and Crimsix have been super successful, but maybe I'm just a little more old-school. I'm not saying that my team would beat the current OpTic team, because that team is like a lightning rod, but this here would be my hall of fame squad.

1. BigTymeR
2. Rambo
3. Scump
4. NaDeSHoT

creating fun content, but nothing too significant at the time. I was really focused on building a business career. That was my calling and what I was super passionate about. I didn't have this huge appetite for YouTube or content creation, so I went off on a different path.

If *Modern Warfare 3* pulled the scene back, *Black Ops 2* catapulted it forward. With this release in November 2012, the community was back on track. It was Treyarch again and David Vonderhaar. Now they were more invested in eSports than ever. In *Black Ops 2,* there was a *CoD* caster mode and a much better heads-up display. They basically built an eSports program around it. If you ask the players, the gun skill, the mechanics, and the balance of the game was all very intuitive. Things just fell into place and it wasn't by accident.

You could tell Treyarch worked hard on the title. They learned a lot from *Black Ops 1* and from watching what was happening in eSports. Think about it. How proud would you be if you made this game and all of a sudden you saw it being played on a grand scale where there were tournaments and the best players in the world competing for money? I'm not a video-game publisher, so I can't say for certain, but knowing that this was all because of the game you created, I would say it's hard not to become passionate about eSports once you see what it can become. I'm sure the team at Treyarch realized the potential. In the end, it was probably a minimal investment on their end to put in these eSports features. They really had nothing to lose. David Vonderhaar is a brilliant dude and he's got his hand on the pulse of the community, so he knows what people want even if they don't realize it yet. The guy just gets it.

At this time, I was the head of the eSports division at Machinima. As a company, we hosted the first tournament of the *Black Ops 2* season—Frag Cup 4. It was held over a weekend in December 2012. HastrO and I were casting the final thirty-two teams who were competing for the $10,000 prize. When putting together a tournament, the organizer has the right to establish his own rules. There isn't some larger governing body that sets the rules. At this early stage, *Black Ops 2* was restricting a bunch of different settings to make it as competitive as possible, but all these crazy new settings really did was water the game down. The big one that comes to mind was the removal of kill streaks, which were synonymous with *Call of Duty*.

Machinima was not just an eSports company like MLG. Machinima was a gaming brand and it was a large gaming brand. Since we were hosting, I said, "I'm going to take a different position on this and take a risk by creating a rule set that is more inclusive to gamers in general and not just eSports." Will the casual *Call of Duty* fan watching this understand why kill streaks aren't on or why they're only playing certain maps and modes? Probably not. I was trying to scale back all those limitations that have been implemented historically so the game could be more accessible to the casual viewer. I wanted to do something unconventional, so the first thing I did was put kill streaks back into the game. I approached it like we had nothing to lose. Why not try it and see what happens?

Well, the community was enraged. People were livid, and if you go back and look up old forum posts, you can see all the mean shit people said to me about it, but I think it worked. Treyarch saw us do this. They saw that it worked and that viewership was up, so they thought there might be something to it. Treyarch had influence, so this led to the use of kill streaks during MLG events for the rest of the *Black Ops 2* season. I'm biased, but I stand behind the fact that we should have kill streaks to some degree in the game and that the publisher should work on making sure that there is balance and fairness to those streaks.

What was really interesting about Frag Cup was that it was the first time NaDeSHoT and Scump teamed up together. Scump had joined during *Modern Warfare 3* and NaDeSHoT had just been bumped up to the main team. What they were about to do as players and personalities would make them two of the biggest names in *Call of Duty*. That was by far the best year *Call of Duty* had ever seen. Not just in terms of success and viewers, but we got it back on track as an eSport. OpTic was leading that charge and about to explode in a big way. OpTic as a team had never been stronger. There was OpTic and then there was everyone else.

17

UMG CHICAGO

NaDeSHoT

knew I was being selfish, but I didn't have a choice. Here I was asking OpTic to drop Rambo and pick me up. If I was going to make a career out of gaming, I had to look out for myself and give myself the best possible chance to succeed.

By the end of 2012, I was making sniper videos, creating YouTube content, and had even played on a few different teams. I was gaining a following and had been talking to Red Bull about a possible sponsorship, but joining the OpTic competitive team was my number one goal. That was what I'd wanted to do from the very beginning. Over the years I'd get a little taste, but it wouldn't last and that was frustrating. Nobody was going to give me a roster spot. I wasn't that kind of player, so I had to go out and get it. There was an opportunity here and I had to take it.

What made this so much harder was that I was good friends with Rambo, but we were very similar players. We played the exact same role on the team and had the exact same mind-set. Some would argue that he was better than me and vice versa. Regardless what people thought, I knew for a fact that if I took his spot, we could definitely win. All I needed were the right players around me. After winning XP, I never felt that I had a chance to prove myself because I was always playing with different combinations of players and hoping we'd be able to win something. That never happened. I had a couple good placings, but what I really needed was a team I could rely on.

Just asking these guys to make a roster move wasn't that easy. I had to be a salesman. I was talking to MerK, Big T, Hector, and Scump individually, trying to sell myself. Scump and I were playing a lot before I joined the roster—mostly online tournaments together. I wasn't the best player in the world, but Scump was. I knew that he was playing with me because I had a pretty big following on my live stream. He wanted to be a part of it, and there's nothing wrong with that. It was a good trade-off for me as well. I think our entire relationship was built around that dynamic. Over time we became better friends, but back then I was using that opportunity to get in his ear. "Let me on the team. I'm as good if not better than Rambo. I think we can do this."

Finally I started to get through to them. My persistence paid off and they all agreed. I was now on the team before the start of the *Black Ops 2* season. That was the first hurdle, but now came the time when I actually had to back up what I was selling. I felt so much pressure to prove that I belonged on this team. I went as hard as possible and played as much as I could. Between online tournaments and practicing every day, I tried to take advantage of every single moment.

This was right before OpTic exploded and became super popular. Our fans at that point were more hard-core and they were upset that we dropped Rambo. Aside from *CoD* XP, I hadn't won any major tournaments, so all I heard was "They're not going to win with NaDeSHoT. They're only doing it because he will make them the most money." There were fans who gave me support, but the vast majority of them looked at it like I was the one who broke up this dream team from *Modern Warfare 3*. This was something I had to cope with every day.

NADESHOT RANKS THE CALL OF DUTY TITLES

NADESHOT

I fell in love with *Call of Duty* during *Call of Duty 4*. I played it twelve hours a day because I enjoyed it so much. It was the simplest *Call of Duty* and the most fun. *Modern Warfare 2* had the same concept and I was playing it during a time when I was just starting to compete on a higher level. *Black Ops 2* makes the list because it was so competitive and so well made, and so much changed for me during that game that I can't keep it off this list.

1. *Call of Duty 4*
2. *Modern Warfare 2*
3. *Black Ops 2*

On the very last weekend of December 2012 was the first LAN of the year at UMG Chicago. All the teams would be there playing this brand-new game and looking to prove that they were the best right out of the gate.

I was filling in for Rambo, so nobody expected me to win, but I knew I would get the blame if things went wrong. This was my time. I had to step up to the plate and win.

When the tournament started, we got off to a great start and blew by everyone. We made it to the finals against CompLexity, who ended up being the most dominant team that year. Remember that this wasn't a huge MLG event. This was a very grassroots LAN setting. The venue was tiny and the two teams were up on this make-shift stage only a couple feet apart. There were no soundproof booths. When the match started, CompLexity immediately took a couple maps off us and started talking an incredible amount of shit. That's all that team ever did.

I could just feel my back up against the wall. We were losing as a team, but in my head, it felt like I was the one having to support us because everyone would point the finger at me if we lost. I wanted to prove them wrong. Slowly, we fought our way back and won the match. In the end, I really think all that pressure the fans put on me (and I know I put a lot of it on myself too) helped me play better. It kind of lit a fire under my ass and gave me more incentive to win. It's really hard to say what would have happened and how I would have played without all those voices trying to tell me that I couldn't do it.

After beating CompLexity, we all went crazy onstage! The tiny venue went nuts. The live stream went nuts. The chat just blew up. After hearing it from CompLexity the entire match, we were yelling back at them. Everything seemed to settle down for a bit, but when I went over to shake their hands, Aches from CompLexity straight up pushed me right there on the main stage in front of everyone. I'm not a confrontational person, but I'm not the type of guy who will just back down and take it when somebody does something like that to me. I got in his face, but I didn't want to do anything stupid that would cost me the Red Bull deal. There was a lot on the line, so I made sure not to lay a hand on him.

Aches has always been my biggest rival. I don't hold a grudge, but my relationship with him always had its ups and downs. We've gotten into arguments on Twitter, and we still go back and forth. I've teamed with him before and respect him tremendously for how much he's won. He's one of the best players in competitive *Call of Duty,* but I'm not the biggest fan of the way he conducts himself. There was a period during *Black Ops 2* and *Ghosts* when CompLexity dominated, but I wish they were more gracious when they won. Every time they won, it just seemed like they got even more cocky and pompous. They had this rude attitude that was hard to swallow, and I'm an opinion-ated person, so this sometimes led to arguments. Now that I'm not competing, it's not that big of a deal, but that team always rubbed me the wrong way.

When things finally died down onstage in Chicago, we got to celebrate the win. It was such a phenomenal feeling not only to win the first event of the year, but to prove to everybody who was doubting me that I belonged on this team. This will always be one of my favorite tournament moments because of that. Now I knew that I wasn't going to get dropped and I finally had that great team around me. Everyone got off my back . . . for a little while at least.

18

THE OPTIC HOUSE

H3CZ

We all saw that NaDeSHoT was developing this cult following on YouTube. Bringing him onto the OpTic eSports team would boost their popularity immediately. NaDeSHoT was one of the only eSports players making videos, so he could have easily become the face of any team. He was also now attracting attention from Red Bull, which was interested in sponsoring him. No other *Call of Duty* eSports player had ever been sponsored in North America, so this was big. I saw Red Bull as a sponsor that would legitimize OpTic and *Call of Duty* as an eSport.

Modern Warfare 3 taught me a lesson about how to survive in this scene. *Call of Duty* is a very strange eSport in that it changes every year with the release of a new game. We have no idea what that game will look like or how it will be perceived. When the scene took a step back because there were no *Modern Warfare 3* LAN tournaments in North America, OpTic didn't have a team competing. This put a damper on things, but it also put me in a bad spot with sponsors. They were looking to me for answers that I didn't have. From that point forward, I made the decision that I was not going to sell tournaments or appearances. I was going to sell OpTic. Instead of telling a sponsor that we could play an eSports event in front of a hundred thousand people, I told them we would give them a hundred thousand views. For that, we didn't even have to leave the house.

We wouldn't be reliant on the success of a particular game or negatively impacted by somebody else's mishaps. We were going to succeed or fail because of us. If the game released that year happened to be a good one, then awesome, but if it wasn't a good game, we were still going to grow. This forced me to make some incredibly difficult decisions that once again centered around NaDeSHoT. One of the hardest things I ever had to do as a team owner came in November of 2012. It was just before the release of *Black Ops 2* when we made the decision to replace Rambo with NaDeSHoT.

Rambo was always considered the most strategic player in all of *Call of Duty*, but he was ineligible for certain tournaments because of where he lived in Canada. NaDeSHoT had filled in for him twice in 2011 already. We then learned that Rambo wasn't going to be eligible for the Frag Cup that would start the *Black Ops 2* season. None of this was his fault. It wasn't fair that Rambo couldn't play. He had worked incredibly hard every single day to become one of the best players only to have those opportunities taken away, but this was an issue that wasn't going away. It disrupted the team and the chemistry, not knowing if he would be eligible, or if we would have to come up with a last-minute replacement. If I could have afforded to have two teams at the time, I would have given that second team to Rambo and they would have been very good. I just wasn't in the position to do that at the time.

This is how we explained it to the fans, but there were other factors completely outside the competitive game that played a role in the decision as well. Growth in *Call of Duty* eSports is determined by viewership, and nobody was making an effort like we were to create an audience. *Call of Duty* needed a hero. It needed somebody in the limelight. We needed to inject the sport with steroids and that meant giving NaDeSHoT a place on the best competitive team in the game.

Normally, I let the team make all the roster decisions, but this was the one time when I intervened and encouraged them to make the switch. BigTymeR, MerK, and Scump understood the bigger picture. We all agreed to do something unconventional that the fans might not initially like, but something that would be the better play in the long run. To me it was a decision that had to be made in order to create the future of this team.

FWIZ'S TAKE

Look, people watch NBA games to see LeBron and Kobe. People watch football to see Tom Brady and Aaron Rodgers. The general public doesn't watch football because of number 78 on the Packers. They don't know who that player is. They know about Aaron Rodgers and who he is on and off the field.

You could no longer be just a really good player and expect notoriety in eSports. You had some pro players who had the personality of a wet carrot. That made it difficult to root for them. On the other hand, you couldn't just be an entertainer and expect to be a good player. Hutch was the perfect example. He was really popular, but he wouldn't even last a minute with pro players.

I never thought like this when I first started, but that moment of realization for me occurred with NaDeSHoT. He was the closest we had seen to being the best of both worlds. NaDeSHoT was a good player and a legitimate pro, but when he joined this team he was not better than the players around him. Luckily, he did have the skill level to hang, so it wasn't a pure marketing decision, but it definitely started a conversation.

I don't know if eSports will ever be able to operate without a content model involved. Here in the U.S., you have to be able to do both, not just rely on being a good player, to be an elite superstar.

Unfortunately, this decision came at the expense of Rambo. The problem was that the fans weren't going to understand this from a business perspective. We couldn't just say, "Hey, guys, due to the fact that NaDeSHoT is so popular, we're going to put him in Rambo's spot to build up a hero in an attempt to win over more fans and attract sponsors to make *Call of Duty* an eSport that people will want to watch." That wouldn't fly.

We didn't lie to the fans when citing Rambo's citizenship issues as the reason, but we weren't completely honest either and that was a mistake. I know now that I should have been more honest and up-front with our fans at the time about why we made the change. Looking back, this was another big lesson I learned as a team owner. It worked out for the best, and I don't think I was wrong, but I could have handled it better.

There was still backlash. Fans attach themselves to players and a lot of them thought we were better off with Rambo. NaDeSHoT received a lot of criticism, and so did I. People thought I made the move because NaDeSHoT was my friend and I was looking out for my buddy. I knew NaDeSHoT would put a lot of pressure on himself, but we didn't know if all of the trash talk would cause him to buckle, or if it would light a fire under him. It bothered him to see people on Twitter saying "You suck" and "I hope they kick you out." It's hard not to let that affect you, but he was always strong mentally. The only person who could bring him down was himself, so he rose to the challenge.

It's not that NaDeSHoT wasn't good. That gets forgotten during discussions like this. He was still a pro player and one of the best, but that doesn't mean he was going to dominate. There is very little that separates a top-ten player from the number one player. That line is incredibly thin and during any given tournament somebody can shine and somebody can fail. It didn't surprise me that he succeeded. I was happy to see him do well and help the team win UMG Chicago because it felt like vindication. He could silence all those people who were quick to use the hashtag #BetterWithRambo. After that first tournament win in Chicago, we proved that we could win with NaDeSHoT. The fans let up, but there was still a boisterous minority that would continue to voice their dissatisfaction when we didn't place well.

The thing that made NaDeSHoT successful on the competitive side was the same thing that made him successful on YouTube—his ability to connect. Every guy thought NaDeSHoT was the best friend he never met. People loved to watch his everyday activity. They wanted to hear what he had to say. So when it came time for him to compete, they were cheering for him. They knew him. There was nobody else in all of eSports who the fans knew, or had access to through social media. The majority of his fans wanted to be there for him no matter if he won or lost.

Lucky for us, *Black Ops 2* was the most popular and exciting game *Call of Duty* had ever seen. It was just so much more fun to watch, and the sport was becoming more popular than ever, so we decided to double down and really take advantage of that growing popularity. As the season progressed into 2013, there was something much bigger in the works: the OpTic House.

Gaming houses have always been around, but not at the level that we were going to do it. Traditionally, a gaming house was a place of work where players went to practice. For me, the OpTic House was going to be a place where the competitive team could practice, but also create content. Yes, the players would be building chemistry while living and practicing together, but for me making videos was always the top priority because without that there would be no audience for eSports. We decided to rent the house, and it's still a toss-up whether or not that was a good move. Owning assets is always better than renting, but we were so young that we couldn't afford to take that leap without knowing where it would lead.

NaDeSHoT, BigTymeR, MerK, and Scump were the four members of the competitive team and would be the first to occupy the OpTic House. This was also an opportunity for all of the others to benefit from NaDeSHoT's popularity. He had such a big following

BIGTYMER ON RAMBO

There is always something you can improve on as a player and I think one of my weaknesses was that I didn't always talk or call out as much as I needed to. A big part of competitive *Call of Duty* is communication. You can do the bare minimum and tell your teammates something simple like, "I saw this guy at the bus," or you could go deeper and say, "This guy is at the bus, I shot him two times, this was his name, and there's two people dead." That gives your team more information and essentially helps them more than it helps you.

I always thought I talked more than I actually did and the reason was because Rambo used to do this for everyone. His objective was to make everyone else around him better. Sometimes his own stats suffered because of that. It was really tough not to have him on the team. I didn't even realize until after Rambo was gone how big of a role he played. That's not a knock on NaDeSHoT at all. NaDeSHoT did a great job filling in and taking over that leadership role, but I had been playing alongside Ray my whole career. We basically came up together, and it was more difficult for me to flourish individually as a player without him. He was a good teammate and a good guy who made me and a lot of other people he played with better.

that I knew his fans would become fans of the others and vice versa. The only way we could fail was if the guys didn't get along . . . which almost happened.

On June 15, 2013, the team house was born. When we stepped into that house, the first thing I told everyone was "You guys typically see each other during events for one weekend a month. It's awesome and you enjoy each other's company, but when you live with someone twenty-four/seven, their mannerisms, cleanliness, or lack of cleanliness, is going to get on your nerves. We're all men here, so if somebody has a problem, let it be known. Don't hold anything back because it will blow up in your faces." Some people listened to that. Some people didn't.

I had no idea what to expect when sticking four dudes under one roof. The worst part of it for me was the mess, and I didn't even live there. NaDeSHoT would leave his food everywhere. He would eat at a station and then just shove his burrito bowl off to the side of the table. This piled up for days and there were fruit flies everywhere. It turned into a disgusting place to live and it wasn't long before we decided to hire a maid. Even then, it was still a mess. What did I really expect? These were nineteen- and twenty-year-old dudes who had been living with their parents up to that point. They were now left to their own devices and fending for themselves. It may have been a huge mess, but it worked.

We saw growth on the very first day we moved into the house. There were fifty thousand people watching across all four players' channels. We didn't have to wait and hope for it to grow. It was immediate. This was the first time *Call of Duty* became one of the top-three channels on Twitch. I still have the screenshots to show how big that move was for our channels. We quickly learned that the fans were interested in the daily lives of the players. Now they could literally be a fly on the wall.

NaDeSHoT was the most prolific when it came to making videos, but Seth was quickly catching up. Seth was developing a reputation for being the best player in the game, but now fans were starting to gravitate toward him as a personality on YouTube. He was talkative and funny, but a little goofy too. NaDeSHoT and Scump fed off each other, and now that they were both a part of OpTic's competitive team, each one was exposed to the other's fan base. It wasn't long before they were the two biggest names, not only in *Call of Duty*, but in all of eSports. What's funny is that they went about it in completely different ways. NaDeSHoT was an entertainer first and Seth was a competitor, but now those paths were starting to intersect and run parallel to each other. It was pretty amazing to be able to watch it all happen.

We were now a part of what I liked to call the new age of eSports athletes. These guys had to be stand-alone individuals and push the boundaries of what any eSport athlete had done in the past. You not only had to focus on competitive gaming, but you also had to focus on making videos and streaming. Once again it was NaDeSHoT who was out in front of everyone else. Not only was he the first guy making videos, but he was also the first guy to live-stream.

Some players don't have it in them to stream and make videos. That's perfectly fine. They're professional players, so they should be paid to be the best. They're not wrong for not wanting to make their lives public. It's not for everyone, especially when you see how hard it is to become a successful personality. Some shied away from the camera. Others dove in. That's not an easy thing to do. Nobody knows how the public will react. You have no way of knowing if you're going to be accepted as an entertainer until you put yourself out there.

BigTymeR was one of the guys who resisted doing YouTube for a long time. He would live-stream a little back when he lived in Arkansas, but even after seeing the success of NaDeSHoT, he still wouldn't fully commit to being an entertainer. His argument was that NFL players didn't have to do what we were doing. He was right, but we weren't in the NFL. We didn't have that status. Competitive *Call of Duty* was not close to being at that level yet. We were still trying to build something, and in order to do that the fans had to know who the players were.

We finally got BigTymeR on board and he made his first video. I think everybody's immediate reaction was the same: What the fuck? How is he this good in front of the camera? Why has he not been doing this the whole time? He was a natural YouTuber, which is so much harder to be than people realize. Once he put his mind to it, he killed it. He knew what people wanted to watch. His first video got a hundred thousand views overnight, which is unheard of. We had NaDeSHoT and Scump, who could push other players' videos, but Will's success wasn't a result of them. He was just that funny. Will had it. He was a YouTube entertainer and nobody knew it because up to that point, he was only about winning tournaments. He didn't need any time to adjust or any help coming out of his shell.

19

MY YOUTUBE CAREER IN A NUTSHELL

BigTymeR

O kay, hang on. Let me start off by saying I was never against making videos—I just had no idea how to do it. How do you even begin doing something like that? There were barely any competitive gamers doing this kind of stuff, so it's not like we had a model to follow. Let's say somebody asked you to start your own personal YouTube channel right now—what would you do today for a video, and every day for the next couple years? See? Not that easy, is it?

We could always tell deep down what H3CZ was trying to build, but it's not like he was pressuring us. There wasn't any kind of quota we had to meet for video making or anything like that. He would say things like "Hey, there is an opportunity here that you're not taking advantage of. There is a way to make a substantial amount of money outside of tournaments." He was right, but with the exception of NaDeSHoT, most of us were late to the game and wasted a lot of time.

When we first moved into the OpTic House in June 2013, we knew that everybody would at least try making YouTube videos, so I was going to give it a shot.

Up to that point I had been solely focused on playing competitively. I didn't even watch much YouTube, so this whole thing was very foreign to me. I probably should have studied up a little more. NaDeSHoT had been doing the sniper thing, and sniping had been big, but I had never been into any of that, so I wasn't going to suddenly make this sniper montage. At the time, it wasn't really proven that competitive game play would even work on YouTube. I knew that I wanted to have fun with it, but I had never tried to be funny on camera before, so I had no idea how people would respond.

My first video really wasn't anything special. There was no planning that went into it. I was just trying to have fun and get a laugh. It was basically a clip that I ripped off my stream from when I was living in Arkansas. Right before I made that video, I was talking to Rambo. He was no longer on OpTic, but we were still good friends, so I was telling him that I had no clue how to get a YouTube channel off the ground. He told me, "Man, you should post that knife rave thing." I just remember him dying laughing during that clip, and laughing is pretty contagious on YouTube. If you can find a video where somebody has a funny laugh, it helps create that positive vibe. Fortunately, it was pretty well received. *Thank God, they like me. I guess I can do this after all.*

It was exhilarating and terrifying at the same time. I had that first one out of the way. I tried something and it worked. Great. The part that scared me the most was having to be consistent and posting a video every single day. That still scares me and I've been doing it for a couple years now. I credit the house and that whole atmosphere for really helping everything grow. NaDeSHoT had already built his audience before moving into the house and was just then starting to take off on YouTube. People had been able to watch us live-stream for a while now, but nobody had ever seen anything like four guys living in a team house. We were able to start making vlogs and videos of us doing everyday stuff instead of just the game-play footage.

THE STORY BEHIND MY VIDEO INTRO

I think I was in a GameBattles match with MerK, NaDeSHoT, and Scumpii when I said the line "wake up, bitch!" Maybe somebody else said it, but it's my chapter and I'll take credit for it. I made a joke like, "That should be my YouTube intro since I don't have one." I started with that line on the first video and people loved it. I had also been trying for the longest time to come up with some kind of outro, but I couldn't think of anything and it annoyed the crap out of me. Eventually, the more I played around with it, the more I found an outro in not having an outro. I don't think it's really necessary to have either.

It took me a long time to find my niche on YouTube. For me, it wasn't until I made a video called "A Day in the Life . . ." when I started to get comfortable in my own skin. I think it ended up with over a half million hits, and for my channel that was really big. Right around that time, I made a couple of different skits. There was one called "The Perfect Valentine's Day Plan" and another one called the "Peyton Manning + Richard Sherman Interview." Both got a lot of attention, though that Peyton Manning–Richard Sherman interview thing was the worst video I ever posted. Somehow it got a lot of views because people thought it was funny. Go figure. Even so, I think the skit ideas helped me realize that there were a lot of different ways to do videos other than making vlogs where I carry around a camera while talking to myself.

I didn't hate doing vlogs, but it's so damn hard to come up with ideas, especially since we were out here in the Chicago suburbs. It wouldn't be so bad if we were in downtown Chicago, where there were people and events going on, but ain't much going on down here in Hoffman Estates. There was one video I made last fall that you might remember called "How to Cook the Perfect Steak." That was something I just came up with out of desperation on the spot. Even filming it, I was like, *This video sucks.* I had no idea how it would do, but for whatever reason people ended up loving it. This made me realize that it doesn't necessarily matter what you're doing if the viewers like the content creator. As long as you're posting something, and it's not just you staring at yourself while you talk at the camera for two minutes (and I have made plenty of videos like that), it normally ends up doing a lot better than you think it's going to. I've found that people tend to gravitate toward the vlogs and the day-in-the-life videos.

This is the reason why the OpTic House is so valuable. We'd wake up in the morning and try to figure out what type of video we were going to shoot that day. This day-to-day creative process is way more stressful than people imagine. Whether it be challenges, skit ideas, or just trying to think of things to pump out that haven't been done before, or taking things that have been done and putting a unique spin on them. It's a handful and it's definitely a mental stress that I wasn't prepared for when I moved in. I'm sitting here right now and I still have no clue what I'm going to do today for a video. And it's not like I have a lot of backup ideas in the saddlebag. Right now I have some skit ideas, but it has to be winter for those. It's mostly a day-to-day thing. It's hectic when you wake up and think, *Crap, I gotta figure out something to shoot today.* On the flip side, it's good in that it keeps you in a creative mood.

I don't want to give you the impression that everything I do is gold. Far from it. There are some misfires. Last year I made an attempt to branch out and create some more diverse content. I took the route of playing new video-game releases like *The Last of Us, Until Dawn,* and *Metal Gear Solid.* For those that haven't seen any of these, fuck you. I'm kidding. Those videos aren't for everyone, as I clearly found out. It's a series of installments where I literally play the game. This allowed me to be consistent, but I discovered that these were also very hit-or-miss depending on the game I was playing. The audience that watches these videos enjoys the personality and commentary behind the games, but they also enjoy watching good games. Shitty games won't get many views, and the fans do a really good job of letting me know when something isn't to their liking.

REAL-LIFE FAN TWEET

"I can't wait for the vlog channel. I personally think the long-ass-drawn-out game plays suck, and I don't mean this in a smartass way as Big T seems to get offended by everything. Just my personal opinion."

I love y'all. But in my defense, there was no YouTuber who was getting views off games like *Metal Gear* and *Mad Max,* because they were so bad. The length of the game also plays a big part in how well these videos do. If you get into a series that has forty or fifty videos, by the time you get to the end, there's nobody watching anymore because it takes such a commitment to follow the story that far. I've decided to stay away from these videos for a while. They might be back by the time you read this book. Who knows? In fact, forget everything I just said and check it out. They're awesome.

If you're playing a good game, these types of videos can work, but you have to be able to take advantage of things like the search engine on YouTube. Our new videos will automatically pop up in the subscription box of our subscribers, but in order to really gain a new audience, what a lot of YouTubers will do is optimize their search results. Back when I was featuring *Until Dawn,* I wanted to figure out what people were typing into YouTube to bring up their search results. What is the most searched item? Is it *"Until Dawn* game play"? Is it *"Until Dawn* part one"? Is it *"Until Dawn* walk-thru"? I'll do various searches to see where my videos pop up. I have to really critique the titles of the videos along with the description and the playlist annotation. Any of these simple little things can get my video above somebody else's, which can result in a snowball effect that gets me on the front page of a search and essentially more views. That builds more subscribers, and then they can check out older videos. There's no algorithm you can type in or anything, but YouTube has done a really good job with their updates and analytic reports, so we can find out exactly where our traffic is coming from—whether it's from our subscribers, related videos, or searches. They help that way, but for the most part you're on your own and it's a dog-eat-dog world.

These weren't the types of things any of us were thinking about when we started because people were coming to our channel specifically for our names. They were finding us, but now I try to be more organized and take more of a professional, businesslike approach. To really make it on YouTube, it takes consistency and originality. Don't take time off. You have to upload a video every day for years (not just days) at a time, and you can't just upload the same thing that a thousand other people are doing. You have to stand out.

A lot of our current success on YouTube has to do with getting in early. We were all lucky to get in when we did. Back when we started, and even two years ago, there was not nearly as much gaming content being pumped out on YouTube. If you're just now trying to start a career on YouTube, and have no background or anything that can get your name out there, it's tough. The guys that started YouTube before us, people that started in 2009 and 2010, those are the ones with five to ten million subscribers and making millions of dollars a year. They've uploaded thousands of videos, so their success is attributed to hard work, but so much of it is about being in the right place at the right time.

It's not like I knew what I was doing. When I go back now to look at my old videos, they just seem so . . . eh. Quality-wise they were pretty awful. My audio and picture quality sucked. We weren't using the best equipment. We could have done a much better job making higher-quality videos. NaDeSHoT was the early advocate of making high-quality videos. He understood because he'd been doing it longer. Scumpii, who has a huge following on YouTube, didn't even get a high-definition camera until recently. He was recording vlogs on his iPhone, and I was doing the same thing. Granted, we were still trying to figure out how this whole thing worked, but having the right camera equipment makes a big difference.

When we moved into the OpTic House, camera equipment was the last thing on our minds. We didn't even have fucking furniture. The OpTic House was like a prison. We joke about it now, but for the first six months we were all sleeping on air mattresses. We never bought anything for the house. It was sort of like an office where we happened to live. It was hectic and I know we got on each other's nerves, but I didn't care. I don't think any of us cared. I was all for moving into the house from the first time we talked about it. Hell, I was living in an apartment back in Arkansas and it was pretty shitty, so the team house was a definite step up for me. I always wanted to take a few years to live outside Arkansas and this seemed like the perfect opportunity. I took time off from college and committed to gaming full-time. I was all in at this point and it was great. We spent the whole day with each other doing anything video-game-related. That definitely helped us bond and gave us something to work toward together. And we were having fun doing it.

20

HOW I SPENT
MY SUMMER VACATION

Scump

Talk of the OpTic House began in the spring of 2013. There was so much we were trying to figure out. Did we nail down the lease? Is everyone on board? It took a ton of planning. While everyone was doing all that, I was back in Pennsylvania still trying to finish high school. This was a monumental, life-changing decision I had to make here. Do I go to college, or do I see how far I can take this pro gaming career and move into the OpTic House? I always planned on going to college and had been accepted to Penn State. I wasn't sure what to do, but I did know that I couldn't do both.

If the *CoD* community had been where it was a year or two earlier, this wouldn't have been much of a decision at all. I'd go to college because there wasn't enough money to be earned from tournaments, so it wasn't worth bypassing school. But once I started streaming and doing YouTube, everything changed. Now money was coming in and I saw that this could be a career. I knew that if I put in the time, I would see results and be able to do this for a living. Isn't that what you go to college to figure out? I asked my mom what she thought I should do and she told me, "Video games aren't going to be there forever. This is a once-in-a-lifetime opportunity. School will always be there if this doesn't pan out. Even if you take a year off, it's not a big deal."

So that's what I did. I decided to forgo college and move into the OpTic House.

I graduated high school in June, and I actually skipped senior week so I could move into the house immediately. The transition was pretty crazy. One week I was in high school and the next week I was in the workforce. That's what I'm gonna call it because the rest of my friends had the summer off before college. I wasn't going to college, so I jumped right into what was basically my full-time job. I had no complaints at the time—I still wouldn't do anything different. I loved what I was doing, and my friends back home were a bunch of idiots anyway, so it's probably good that I didn't stick around for senior week. It turns out that I didn't miss anything.

Living in the OpTic House was definitely a different experience. As soon as we got there, it kind of sucked. There was nothing in the house. It didn't feel like home—it was strictly a workplace. There was nowhere to relax. We didn't even have a TV. There were five setups in the main living room, and it got super hot in there. The first six months were awful and I'm sure everyone there would tell you that. This also meant that there were literally no distractions, so it just turned into this crazy grind. We'd make a YouTube video, stream for eight hours, and go to sleep. But we didn't even have beds. We all slept on air mattresses. There was no time to wind down before we had to do it all over again the next day.

Hey, I'm not complaining. As awful as I might have made this sound, I don't think anybody second-guessed the decision to move into the house. We wanted it to work, and it was probably a good thing that there was nothing else for us to do. We were in the moment, and watching our channels grow was pretty exciting.

The reason everything was different in 2013 was because of *Black Ops 2*. This was just a really well-made game. It was the best competi-

DON'T BLAME ME!

That was the way they chose to live. I had to take the role of a parent. I could tell them what needed to be done, but I couldn't do it for them. I told them they needed to buy necessities like furniture, but they chose not to do those things. They chose to sleep and work, which I could respect. In the end, I always tried to make sure that I didn't do anything that would hinder their growth or make it hard for them when they did venture out into the workforce. If they were going to live here, they had to fend for themselves.

—H3CZ

tive *Call of Duty* so far—some people would call it the best *Call of Duty* period. From a spectator standpoint, it was really fun to watch. The score streaks in it were particularly fun. If somebody went on a sick streak, they got rewarded and could actually use their score streak against you, unlike most *Call of Duty* games, where score streaks weren't allowed at all. So even if you were on a seven-kill streak in any other game, it wouldn't matter, but in *Black Ops 2* you'd get rewarded. Some of the playmaking potential with those streaks sparked people's interest. Say we were playing Capture the Flag and the other team was running your flag, but you had a lightning strike in your back pocket with thirty seconds left in the game. You could now bomb their team and it would stop the flag completely. That gave you a chance to get back into the game. In most other games you'd simply lose. This was just one of the really cool features they added.

I couldn't wait to play it on LAN. Whenever a new game comes out, everyone's first instinct is to "learn, learn, learn" and grind the game until you can't play anymore. Learn as much as you can as fast as you can so you can get ahead of the competition. The teams that know *Call of Duty,* and are good at *Call of Duty,* are the first ones to learn everything. Everyone was excited about that first LAN tournament of the year at UMG Chicago. That would be the proving ground where we'd find out who was going to be the best. This was probably the most excited I've ever been about a tournament, and like NaDe-SHoT just told you, we ended up winning, so that got everything off to a great start.

This was when the Green Wall fan base grew. Whenever we'd go to tournaments, we started to get recognized and see a ridiculous number of Green Wall T-shirts in the crowd. Even to this day it's the same thing. We have a great group of fans that we built through YouTube and streaming. It was nice to see people cheering for you and supporting you, but it was also strange to me at first. At these events we couldn't go too far without having to sign autographs

WHY WAS BLACK OPS 2 SO POPULAR?

Before *Black Ops 2*, the reason competitive *Call of Duty* had such a hard time catching on was that if you didn't already know about competitive *Call of Duty*, it was impossible to just sit down and watch it. It wasn't like football, where you could turn on a game and, without knowing anything about the game, still get a pretty good idea what's going on. If you didn't know *Call of Duty*, you'd have no idea what you were looking at. I think it was the developer support from Treyarch that turned things around. This was an idea you can chalk up to David Vonderhaar. He attended a few of the *Black Ops 1* tournaments in 2011. He would sit down and talk to us about what we needed, what would make the game better, and also what would make it more competitive and spectator-friendly. He was the first developer who took that to heart and implemented it into the game.

—BigTymeR

or something. Hearing "Oh crap, there's Scumpii!" It was weird. I never experienced this before in my life and now I was suddenly "that guy." Growing up as a kid playing video games, I never imagined that I'd be signing autographs. Seeing fans shaking when they come up to you is still something I have a hard time wrapping my head around.

This kind of attention wasn't just new for us. It was new for *Call of Duty*. I think we paved the way for future competitive players, but it wasn't easy. Other pros were only focused on playing competitively and going to tournaments, but we were also making videos and live-streaming at the same time. We revolutionized *Call of Duty* because we made it an actual career option for these players. If you're not lazy and you have the drive to start producing content, there's no reason why you can't do both. We proved that it could work. Only a year earlier, me and Matt were making videos and streaming for fun. There wasn't a whole lot of money to be made. Suddenly, with all the popularity surrounding *Black Ops 2*, creating content could make you financially stable. We were lucky because we had already found our niche and had that strong base in place when everything blew up. We got in the game early. It gave us a great safety net, but it all happened so fast.

Without fail, eight months into every single *Call of Duty* season, I get that feeling, *Oh my gosh, I've played this game for so long and seen it all thousands and thousands of times before*. It's hard not to get burned out. We've all been playing this one game eight hours a day for months at a time. You also have to take into account that we've all been playing *Call of Duty* for years at this point, so of course there were times when I've just been super fed up and bored with the game. This didn't happen with *Black Ops 2*. I still hop on to play this game from time to time and it's almost three years old. I never got tired of that game and I think it's the best *Call of Duty* ever made.

Over the course of 2013, I never got sick of playing *Black Ops 2*, but we ran into a much different problem. I'm gonna come right out and say it. This season was really difficult because everybody was so focused on producing content. It was hard to find that balance between creating content and scrimming. From a competitive standpoint . . . eh, we probably got worse after we moved into the house. We were all so focused on streaming and YouTube that it changed our mind-set. We still cared about the competitive *Call of Duty* side, but it wasn't the top priority and it showed in our placings. Some nights we couldn't get to practice because we were already live-streaming. Sometimes we were making YouTube videos, so we didn't want to watch film, or we were in league play on live stream with our subscribers, so we didn't want to do anything else. In the end, it wasn't YouTube and Twitch that set us back. It was more us not wanting to practice because we were so busy with everything else.

I admit that I could have been so much better this season. I should have been better, but I really wasn't prepared for any of this. None of us were, and in all fairness I can't imagine anyone being able to anticipate what was happening. There were stretches during the *Black Ops 2* season when I didn't play the game as much as I should have. There were moments where it showed. When the game first came out, I was on and killing it, but I would fall off later in the season. Then I'd pick back up when *Call of Duty* Championships rolled around and once again be at the top of my game. It was a very streaky season for me and when I didn't put the time in it showed.

When I did put forth the effort, I always thought of myself as one of the best players in the game. I was blessed with good genes. I have really good motor skills, reaction time, and hand-eye coordination. This set me apart, but it wasn't everything. It couldn't be. My competitive sports background taught me how important it was to outwork everyone else. I like to think that I always made smart in-game decisions even though a lot of people didn't think this was the case. My reaction time made up for some of the mistakes that I did make, but I could never rely on that alone. All the pros can shoot straight and predict what you're going to do. At that level, it comes down to who can predict better, make smarter plays, and help the team. That's why I always chuckle when I hear people say that I'm

SCUMP RANKS THE CALL OF DUTY TITLES

Modern Warfare 2 is probably my all-time favorite *CoD*. This was the game I was playing when I was coming up and trying to make a name for myself. Looking back, that was actually what made this game so fun. While playing against better players I was able to see myself slowly getting better in small increments. That was just so incredibly rewarding. I also really enjoy *Advanced Warfare* even though a lot of people in the community don't. I'm probably the only one with this game on their list.

1. *Modern Warfare 2*
2. *Black Ops 2*
3. *Advanced Warfare*
4. *Ghosts*

not a smart player and rely only on gun skill. When people say that, it's clear that they don't know what they're talking about.

I was always confident in myself as a player, but it's not like I didn't have anything to learn. I had weak spots in my game and I knew about them. I had always been fundamentally sound in the respawn game types. Back during *Black Ops 2,* what I needed to improve on was my SnD. Search and Destroy was always my weak spot. That was hard for me because I was so good at respawn and was always so "go, go, go" that trying to slow myself down to play SnD was difficult. Things happen so much slower, and with one life, you have to be so much more careful and take precautions. Opponents were thinking about their moves while I was in that respawn mind-set. It often came back to bite me in the butt. That's the type of player I was. I always had it in my head to play as aggressive as I possibly could, so it took a while to learn how to slow down. I slipped into a weird rut, and I was constantly trying to tell myself how I should be playing, so it took some time.

The *Black Ops 2* season got off to a good start, but after that win in Chicago, things started to go downhill. We had some decent placings. We were always in contention and right there near the top, but we weren't winning any tournaments. Things got worse when we made the decision to drop MerK from the roster. He had been around for so long and was the heart of the team. I had played with him for a year and a half, so it was weird for him to suddenly be gone. I think it was a difficult time for MerK personally. I don't know if it was the pressure or the spotlight or being in the house or whatever. You'll have to ask him, but it just wasn't a good time for any of us and it definitely wasn't an easy decision to make.

MerK was good, but he wasn't a flashy player. We were never the flashy team. We were the fundamentally sound crew with smart *Call of Duty* veterans like BigTymeR. That's why we ended up picking JKap to replace MerK. He was a flashy top-tier player. It was a breath of fresh air. It was something new and it motivated me to better myself as a player and go as hard as I could.

Our first tournament with JKap was Gfinity 2 in London, where we placed ninth. Up to this point, I had never placed lower than sixth. If there was one tournament that I could go back and play again, it would be that one. We've gone on to place lower, but I still refer to this as the biggest blemish on my *Call of Duty* career. I really can't explain what happened to us. The team just fell apart. It was like we forgot how to play Hardpoint. When we left the arena after we lost, I didn't even go out with the team to dinner. I just went back to the hotel and slept. I didn't want to be around anyone.

I wasn't used to losing. We were coming off the *MW3* season where we never finished outside the top two, and even then I hated to finish second. I hated losing more than I enjoyed winning. I had that Ricky Bobby mentality where if I wasn't first I was last. The fans seemed to think that way too and it felt like we would get flak every time we didn't win a tournament. I don't think that was always fair, but in the case of Gfinity, all the criticism was totally deserved. What made this so frustrating was that we practiced so much. We had been winning online scrims. We were beating CompLexity, EnVyUs, and all the top teams online. Once we got to the event, we didn't execute.

I don't know if our confidence took away from our intensity or what, but that was an incredibly long flight back from London.

In the end, that roster change didn't generate the results we were expecting. We had some bright spots, but we didn't end up winning any more tournaments during *Black Ops 2*, and winning was the most important thing. I don't know if it was a chemistry issue or the fans being upset with us on social media. Just like when we replaced Rambo, the haters were coming out of the woodwork to say that we shouldn't have dropped MerK because he was such a big part of the team for so long. We took the blame and a lot of fans looked at us as the bad guys, but we were doing what we thought was best for the team and gave us the best opportunity to win. Looking back, it sort of backfired.

What none of us knew was that things were about to get so much worse when *Call of Duty: Ghosts* was released in November 2013.

PART 5

GHOSTS

21

HYPERGROWTH

H3CZ

Just because you become a member of OpTic doesn't mean that you get to relax. Joining OpTic isn't the goal. Joining OpTic is when you start over. Now you have to work your ass off because now you have the opportunity to experience the payoff. OpTic gives you the chance to reach that goal.

We wanted the members of OpTic to wake up and prepare a video for their YouTube channel every single day. We wanted them to spend seven to eight hours live-streaming. Then, after that, they would go into the editing portion of that video to get it ready for upload. Not only did they have to practice, but they had to be their own entertainer, producer, director, editor, and filmmaker. Those that played competitive *Call of Duty* had to make room to practice and travel. It was like a twelve-hour job every single day and it's not easy to balance all of those responsibilities. No other pro teams were grinding like this, but we were good at making it a rule.

Yes, everything that was going on in 2013 was a distraction to the four guys in the house. This was an example of two worlds colliding. We have always been a video-game entertainment company that dabbled in eSports. Content creation has always been at the top of my list because entertainment was what we were selling. Was trying to build an audience distracting for the competitive players? Yes. But did it work? Absolutely. I had a vision and nothing was going to get me to change course, but I can only imagine how frustrating it was for the players. I know I was distracting them a lot. I was putting pressure on them not only to win, but also to become personalities.

I had my selfish reasons. I wanted to see the company grow, but I also cared about the success of the players. They were the ones forgoing college and putting their lives on hold to pursue this dream. I wanted to put them in the best possible position to be successful, and these were the types of things they needed to be doing to make a career in video-game entertainment. It was important to me that the players be able to restart their lives if this all went south. So if competitive *Call of Duty* didn't work out, at least they'd have a YouTube channel where they could earn a good living while deciding whether to go back to school or find a career.

You can only play so much *Call of Duty*. At the same time, there is only so much *Call of Duty* content you can create. Expanding and broadening the audience also meant playing different games. I would constantly tell them, "I know *Call of Duty* is your job, but try a different game. Play *Minecraft*. There's a huge audience in *Minecraft* and you better believe that a lot of your fans like it." Once again, the guys in the house were reluctant at first. Even NaDeSHoT, who was really good at being in front of a camera at a certain time every single day, didn't want to get on board with *Minecraft*.

What I decided to do was wake up really early one day, answer whatever e-mails I had, and then drive over to the OpTic House. I sat down, turned on my live stream, and played *Minecraft*. By the time the guys rolled out of bed, they saw that I had ten thousand people watching the stream and were like, "What the hell? Why are people watching you play this Lego game?" Little by little I introduced them to *Minecraft*. BigTymeR was the first one to play and then NaDeSHoT hopped in. From that point it was on. The story lines behind what we were doing in that game exploded. People were super entertained by what was happening in the game. For me it was always about content creation. I didn't care what the vehicle was. I didn't care if it was a sniping video, competitive *Call of Duty*, or a *Minecraft* video. I didn't care.

The downside was that the fans would say that *Minecraft*, and

THE OLD MEN OF OPTIC

During *Ghosts*, I wanted to play with OpTicJ again. I was thinking of playing doubles on GameBattles. He was interested and wanted us to call ourselves Menudo after the eighties Puerto Rican boy band (and also J's favorite Mexican dish). "No, we always call ourselves that. Let's call ourselves the Old Men of OpTic." Then we decided to make a team, so we invited Fwiz, Di3seL, and Hutch because they all used to be in OpTic. Every night we would play and live-stream the games. Granted, we would always lose, but the fans were loving it. We had known each other for so long that we didn't hold back anything. We'd talk shit to each other the whole time. We quickly became the second-most-watched *Call of Duty* team next to the main competitive team.

Not everyone could make it every night, so we'd pick up random people from the community. One of the guys who always filled in was Pamaj because he was in OpTic at one point as a sniper. We'd pick on him about how he turned his back on us, and how he'd never be allowed back in. Soon he became one of the members. It was a fun time. We were hanging out with our friends and playing a game we all loved. It brought back memories from when we first started to play together during *Call of Duty 4*. We have since stopped. *Advanced Warfare* was a little too fast for us, but we have high hopes that the Old Men of OpTic will be back for *Black Ops 3*, so keep an eye out.

branching out, was the reason why the players were losing tournaments. "Less *Minecraft*, more *Call of Duty*" was what we constantly heard from the fans. In the background, I'd be whispering to the players to keep playing *Minecraft* and to keep expanding. It definitely wasn't easy for the players because they were on the front line getting yelled at by the fans while I was in the background yelling at them to do the complete opposite.

Believe it or not, it wasn't all about expansion with me. I also had to make sacrifices, and there was one sacrifice in particular that was hard because it was so close to my heart. While the competitive team was getting all this attention, the sniping team had gone in a direction that was much different from my original vision. They had ballooned to over fifteen members and weren't involved with the fans or with each other like I had hoped. I first noticed it when talking to OpTic Kay at Gfinity. He was a cool dude, but I realized that I didn't know him at all. I felt distant. I admit that it's partly my fault and I lost sight of this when I started focusing on the competitive side of OpTic.

DTreats had already left a few years earlier. He was never a big fan of us stepping into the competitive scene. Maybe he felt that his position on the team was threatened. He saw that we were going in a direction that he didn't agree with, so he decided to step away. I don't blame him. We set out to do one thing and then we switched over and started doing something new. It wasn't fair to him or the other snipers.

In the meantime, the current OpTic snipers had become inactive. Their job was to create content and make sure that there were always videos readily available to upload to the OpTic Nation channel. That wasn't happening. They were just happy playing games and acting as though they were a part of OpTic without living the "work your ass off or get the fuck out" philosophy. I'd hear excuses like "I'm working on a montage and it takes time because it's not just a regular video." I'd give them options and tell them, "You still need to create content. Why don't you do a commentary? Why don't you make a vlog? Why don't you do something to fill that void so we can upload something?"

I told them this for months, but they were riding the coattails of NaDeSHoT, BigTymeR, MerK, and Seth, who were living in the house and immensely popular. The snipers weren't pulling their own weight and I got fed up, so in September of 2013, I dropped the entire sniping roster. I always had the intention of bringing back the sniper team, but it never really worked out. I don't want to fall into that same pattern and have to relive it again.

It was time to focus more on competitive *Call of Duty*. We grew tremendously during *Black Ops 2,* but we had a very stressful competitive season. This carried over into *Ghosts,* but because of personalities like NaDeSHoT and Scump, we were still the fan favorite. We were underdogs in every single tournament, but had the following of the number one team in the world. The teams that were successful and winning at this time were overshadowed by the Green Wall. It was the other pros and their fans who were most upset about what we were doing. They felt like OpTic was growing and being rewarded for losing. I could understand that. That should bother them. They would beat us and we were the ones becoming more successful. How could that happen? In spite of the criticism, we knew that we were still helping the other pros. They may have hated us, but we were creating this scene where they too would be able to thrive.

You can only rely on being popular for so long before the fans demand results. Things weren't working and the chemistry was off. NaDeSHoT and Scump were starting to get on each other's nerves while living under the same roof at the OpTic House. Considering how competitive each of them was, it was almost inevitable. They would argue more and more. A few times I actually had to step in to say, "Dudes, you guys need to stop bickering because one of you is going to say something really mean to the other and not be able to take it back."

There was a competition going on at the house where everyone would get up early to start their stream so they could get more viewers. One morning they each sat down at the same time and decided to make a video together. I was sitting at my station right behind them and was waiting for something to go wrong. Sure enough, Scump got this amazing game play, but NaDeSHoT also had an incredible game. They each wanted to upload their game play and this led to a huge fight. They got right in each other's face. And it was the stupidest argument. They had two different game plays, so they could have each uploaded their own video. Scumpii got so mad he punched a hole in the door.

MY SIDE OF THE STORY

Yeah, that's pretty much how it happened. That was back when I worked out a lot, so people would joke that I was 'roid raging. It was childish, I know that, but I will say that we couldn't just upload the same video. Why would you guys want to watch the same game from a different perspective? Tell me if I'm wrong. We were playing league play on *Black Ops 2* and the plan was to use the game we did the best in. Simple, right? The problem was that we both did well in the same exact game. He went 32–2 and I dropped the swarm. We couldn't each upload it. That doesn't make any sense.

—Scump

I don't agree, but whatever. I was scared that we were starting to look like an unstable team. We weren't there yet, but it was about to get really bad.

We were in control when we made the decision to drop Rambo and MerK. The fans didn't like it, but these were our decisions and we did what was best for the team. Now I was starting to feel like I was on the receiving end of bad news when BigTymeR approached me to say that he didn't want to play competitively anymore. It wasn't a surprise. You could see it coming. When someone's heart isn't in the game anymore, you can tell. BigTymeR was just burned out. I understood that and supported his decision. To this day, he doesn't really want anything to do with the competitive scene. He doesn't seem all that interested in going to events. I never asked Will why he retired. Maybe I will today, but it's his decision and he shouldn't have to answer to me. People have different reasons, but I think it's more private when you're a competitor, and it should probably stay that way.

22

ALL GOOD THINGS MUST END

BigTymeR

first started thinking about retiring in the summer of 2013—about three-quarters of the way through the *Black Ops 2* season. I wanted to focus more on YouTube, and people were telling me, "Oh, you could be huge on YouTube." "You have the personality." "You should go for it." I didn't know how popular I'd be as a content creator if I wasn't playing competitively anymore. I'd always sneak in questions on stream to try to ease my mind: "Would you guys watch me play *Madden,* or any single-player games?" We were also experimenting with other videos, and saw that our videos that had nothing to do with *CoD* would do just as well as, if not better than, our *Call of Duty* videos.

Then *Ghosts* came out and everybody fucking hated it. I was not a fan of that game and that just pushed me even closer to retiring.

The competitive season started at the end of 2013 and everything just got so much worse. We were frustrated when we were placing second or third during *Black Ops 2.* Now in *Ghosts* we were placing like thirteenth. That just wasn't acceptable. And the amount of comments and hate we were getting on social media was just ridiculous. It was awful and suddenly that *Black Ops 2* season didn't look so bad. Overall, the tournaments weren't getting viewership and people were calling this the death of *Call of Duty*. If we were winning, I think it might have been different for me. This was a dark time, and it was pretty much everything piling up that made me want to pull the plug. It's tough going into a tournament and thinking, *Oh crap, if we don't win people are going to hate us.* That's just a terrible mind-set to have and that's how we all felt at the time because we'd experienced it for the past three or four tournaments.

The community was also very different. It was so much more competitive and the players were much better than when I first started. During games like *Modern Warfare 3,* when there wasn't much money to be made, some of the older players on other teams weren't really giving it their all. Now, when everyone saw the scene starting to build and the prize money getting bigger and bigger, those old-school players came back to make another push. Combine this with all these new guys coming up and the competition just exploded.

I'm not making excuses or saying that we couldn't compete. We were definitely capable and we should have been one of the best teams that year, but it just didn't happen. What all this new competition meant was that we had to practice so much more. What people don't really understand about competitive *Call of Duty* is the amount of time it takes to continue being the best. You have to grind the game over and over and over and over again. It's a 24-7 endeavor. You're playing tournaments on GameBattles, scrimming with your team, playing late-night tournaments, and it doesn't leave any room for much else. And when your heart is not in it anymore and you're burned out, that's a difficult commitment to make.

I finally decided to tell Hector when he came over to the house one day in December 2013. I told him straight up that UMG Philadelphia in January of 2014 would be my last tournament. That conversation went surprisingly well. He was actually scared that I wanted to move out of the house and drop everything completely. "Absolutely not," I told him. That was the furthest thing from my mind. In fact, I wanted to do the opposite. I wanted to focus on YouTube and live stream and help build my channel. He was all for it and was actually the biggest supporter of me at the time. One love, Hector!

BIGTYMER'S FAVORITE TOURNAMENT MOMENT

This is kind of a depressing section, so we're going to liven it up with some happy memories. Ironically, one of my all-time favorite tournament memories occurred right before I started to think about retiring. During *Black Ops 2,* the community sort of tried to pit OpTic against CompLexity just because we were in the finals of a lot of tournaments. We were known as the nice guys that everybody wanted to watch and CompLexity was really good at playing the role of the villain. They would talk shit to everyone, but were also able to back it up. We were the team everyone liked to root for and they were the team everyone loved to hate. This was the closest we had to a rivalry at the time and it was good for the sport.

This was *CoD* Champs for *Black Ops 2* in April of 2013. It was held at the Palladium in Hollywood. We were playing against CompLexity to see who would continue on to Sunday. The score was 2–2 in a best of five and we were playing the last game in a Search and Destroy match. We couldn't make simple mistakes. I was on top of the leader board at the time—I had like twelve or thirteen kills going into the last round. It was a $20,000 match and we ended up clutching in the last second. Scump had some amazing kill combination to win the game. That sent us on to Sunday and we ended up placing third. We were really good at getting second and third that year. This was also the first tournament that my family came to watch. My mom and two of my aunts were able to make it out there.

I don't know where I'd rank myself on the list of the best players in *Call of Duty*. Too often when people argue about who the best players are, they only look at the stats. Who got the most kills? But if you ask any top *Call of Duty* players, they'll tell you that there are a lot of things that don't show up on the scoreboard that could make or break a game.

Let's say three of your teammates are on one side of the map and you're lopsided. If you have the awareness to go to the other side, wait for your teammates to get picked off, and spawn them closer to your flag, you've suddenly managed to stop a flag score. Not everyone picks up on those types of things, but those were the things that I think I was really good at. Maybe people didn't consider me the best individually skilled player in the game, but when trying to form a 4v4 team where all you wanna do is win the game, then I was one of the first people they'd think of.

There are a lot of one-dimensional players in *Call of Duty*. Still to this day there are people who will stay away from the objectives in certain game modes, or players that will only go for the objective because they're not comfortable slaying. I think what really helped me stand out, regardless of who my teammates were at the time, was that I was good at doing all of that stuff, so I could compensate for what my teammates at the time were not good at doing. I could pick up the slack and this was one of the reasons why I was successful.

I don't want you to think I was miserable the whole time and hated playing. It was always fun for me back when I was sixteen or seventeen. I wouldn't have done it if I didn't love it, but some things in life run their course. And sometimes you wanna play a different game. There are maybe four or five people who were around when I first started that still compete for the top eight. There might be a lot more guys still playing who are nowhere near as good, but most of them have moved on, or gone back to college. Rambo used his playing career and took it to the next level by transitioning into game development. You'll see a few guys go the *CoD* commentary route when they've retired from playing, but most of them end up dropping out of the scene completely.

BIGTYMER'S FAVORITE GAMES OF THE YEAR

I've really gotten into the horror genre this year. I did an *Until Dawn* walk-thru on the channel and that was fun. I don't know. I'm trying to be more of a real gamer. I played so much *Call of Duty* growing up that I didn't get a chance to play many other games. Because of that, I don't even call myself a gamer since there's so much out there that I haven't experienced. But continuing with the list, I liked *Forza* and played that a lot on stream. I kind of want to race cars one day. Me and Ian are talking about joining one of those K-1 speed leagues for competitive go-karts. *Madden* is another game I've been playing a lot. I guess this isn't really much of a true-to-form list. It really depends on when you ask me, but these are the games I had the most fun playing this year.

1. *Until Dawn*
2. *The Last of Us*
3. *Forza*
4. *Madden*

After I retired, the plan was to coach the team through a few tournaments, but that never happened because MLG started banning the use of coaches. I don't know why, but it was something about people in the stands watching the projectors and sending signals to coaches to tell them what was going on with the other teams. So when you're playing Search and Destroy, someone in the crowd could signal to a coach to let him know what bomb site the other team was going to and he could relay that to the players. My coaching career never really got started, but that was okay because I didn't have a whole lot to gain. It's not like I was going to take prize money from the players. Since I've retired, it's been all about YouTube. It may be hard, but I just really love doing it. Content creation is my road map for the next couple of years.

23

MY OWN PERSONAL GRIND

MiDNiTE

I can totally understand why Big T decided to retire. I never played competitively, but I know plenty of people who do, so I understand how much sacrifice it requires. Those guys are under so much pressure, and people like BigTymeR and NaDeSHoT take the blame when they lose. NaDeSHoT especially would be the scapegoat and I can't imagine what that feels like.

Even when you absolutely love what you do, it's possible to get burned out. It was right around this same time in 2014, during *Call of Duty: Ghosts,* when I hit a wall of my own for the very first time. I was struggling to come up with new content. The game was getting old. It was popular when it was first released, but this was the quickest I'd ever seen the fans lose interest in a game. I don't know if it was because the game catered to a slow play style or what, but the scene fizzled and the fans felt like they had seen everything. This made it difficult to come up with content.

What I try to do in these situations is live-stream more. I can get myself out there that way. In the fall of every year, there is typically a lull before the release of a new game. Usually at this point, I either have to make really unique *Call of Duty* content or entertain people other ways through things like daily vlogs. I'd love to play other games, but I've branded myself as a *Call of Duty* player over the last five years and that's the reason why people subscribe to my channel. If I suddenly start playing other games, some people will literally unsubscribe. I have to be careful because I know that *Call of Duty* videos are what get me more views. There is a fine line that you have to learn to walk. How can I give the subscribers content they want to watch while also staying fresh and making videos that differentiate me? The one thing I can't do is stop, and a lot of YouTubers learn this the hard way. It's so easy to get complacent when you see your channel grow, but I know there will always be somebody out there who would kill to be in my position.

When I first joined OpTic in 2010, my channel had only eighty-six subscribers. By the end of that first month, I had reached ten thousand. At the time of *Ghosts,* I was nearing five hundred thousand. At first it's great, but I wasn't prepared for any of this. I thought I could relax because my channel was finally where I wanted it to be, but I quickly discovered this was the worst thing I could do. I've seen channels go down as quickly as they went up.

I'd try to check out what the other *Call of Duty* YouTubers were doing even though I didn't get to watch a whole lot because I was so busy doing my own thing. This was another double-edged sword. I didn't want to be influenced so much that I was ripping off another style. That wouldn't help me. Everyone has their own style, but there were things that I obviously picked up along the way. A lot of times it's the little things that make the biggest difference. I know I really liked how Mr Sark made those little edits in his videos. It made it fun; like we were all in on the joke. I've tried to do more stuff like that, but not imitate him so people could call me out for ripping him off.

Vlogging has been big on YouTube for years, so it's no real surprise that it caught on within the gaming community. Recently, people started talking about Casey Neistat. Since he has a filmmaking background, his videos look totally different from anyone else's in the space, but what I personally picked up on from someone like Casey was how to be more efficient. So let's say I was vlogging during a car ride to the mall. Instead of talking over an entire ten-minute car ride, I might edit it down so I only show a couple seconds of the car ride. The edited footage gives the illusion that time is passing. There's always something else to learn, or a new way you can go about doing things so you don't get stuck in your ways.

THE STORY BEHIND MY YOUTUBE INTRO

I was just randomly playing with my friends on *Modern Warfare 2* and we were talking about something—I don't even remember what, but I said, "What's up, bros and hos." I then started joking about making it my intro. They were like, "You should! It's so funny." That was never my intention, but okay. I started doing it and it kind of caught on, so I stuck with it. Though right now I really want to change it up, but I have no idea what to change it to. I don't even know if people would notice or care if I suddenly changed my intro. People don't seem to like the long drawn-out intros anymore either—they just want you to get to the point.

The one thing that has always set me apart from the pack was the obvious fact that I was a girl. I liked to think that I was a lot different from most of the other girls in the community. I never wanted to follow that traditional girl gamer style where I'd wear a push-up bra and collect donations like a cam girl. I personally never had a problem with anyone who did that. That was their business. They were hustling and there was a market for that sexy girl gamer, but it was never something that worked for me. I always wanted it to be about the game. That's what was important to me. If I suddenly tried to exploit my sexuality, I might be able to make a lot more money, but I'd be attracting the wrong kind of attention. That's not what I'm in it for.

There has always been sexism. This is a male-dominated space with mostly guys posting and mostly guys watching. But I don't think it was ever as bad as people made it seem. There was never a specific opportunity that I missed out on because I was a girl, but the one criticism I hear all the time is that the only reason I got into OpTic is because I was a girl. There's a group out there who don't take me seriously, or for some reason think what I do doesn't matter as much because I have boobs. That has always bothered me.

I can't deny that being a girl gamer does have its advantages. I always got a lot of interview requests and received attention at events. I've appeared in the *Guardian, Forbes,* and a few other publications. I knew that I was getting that attention specifically because I was a girl. That's fine. A lot of times these publications want to see what it's like to be a girl in the community and I'm happy to provide that perspective, but I always tried to keep it as real as I could. I was never trying to be a role model or anything, but I did want to show people that there was a way to do it without having to exploit your sexuality. That was important to me.

I never wanted to be defined by my sexual preferences. I never liked labels and I hated being called a lesbian or bisexual. To me, love is love. It doesn't matter if you date guys or girls, it's still love to me. Still, this has always been a part of my life, so I have shared things at times. I don't frequently talk about it, but part of being a personality involves so much more than playing the actual game. I feel that if I don't share this side of me, I won't be opening up the way that I need to. You can't dance around the truth or people will notice. You have to be honest and you have to be yourself. People seem to either really like me or they really don't, and the people who do like me help to make my little slice of the Internet so much better. It took me a long time to be completely comfortable opening up. Since it was so personal, I was worried about rejection, but I realized that people were

BAD ASS GIRL GAMERS

When I first joined OpTic, I created this series called *Bad Ass Girl Gamers* where I interviewed some of the girls in the industry and put it over game-play footage. I had met so many cool women along the way who were gamers just as much as any guy. There was no reason for them to be discriminated against. They loved games. They were good at games. Some of the women I played with were even better than the guys. The ultimate goal was to break that stigma surrounding girl gamers, and basically all stigmas, to show that gamers aren't just these guys locked away in their mom's basement. That's why I did the series.

I was pretty much raised by a single mother who was entrepreneurial and owned her own company. I've always been a little more sensitive to the issue and think it's important that we don't sexualize women in the gaming industry. Last year, I was one of the industry leaders invited to do a panel in the Roosevelt Room at the White House. We discussed how to empower women in this industry. There were some pretty amazing people there and we talked about what we could do as a group to make improvements. We discussed everything from equal opportunity jobs to how women were treated online and even about not sexualizing women as characters in the actual games. I've always had a passion to expose this as an issue and feel that I could still do more.

—Fwiz

more attracted to someone who was genuine. You just have to dive in and put yourself out there.

Last summer I had this idea to film a vlog from the gay pride festival. I had gone every year, but I had never filmed it before. I thought I'd give it a shot because maybe some people would like to see that part of my life. I made sure not to show anything close to being offensive. I focused mostly on the parade and some of the other cool ff going on. Once I posted this video, it ignited a crazy war in the comments. A lot of people were not okay with this subject. I realize a lot of the fans are really young and have a much different point of view, but what was weird was that I actually saw a decrease in subscribers for the first time in the history of my channel.

I was completely fine with that. I would rather weed out those people. If they don't enjoy that part of my life, I'm not going to force them to watch it. There were some nasty comments, but the comments weren't all negative. I got a lot of support, and there were a lot more positive comments than there was criticism, but the criticism was something that I was not expecting.

It took me a very long time before I learned how to handle criticism. Whenever someone would say something negative or call me a name, my first instinct was to defend myself. There was nothing wrong with that, but I often took an immature approach. I would get into fights on Twitter all the time. Hector finally had to tell me, "You just have to ignore them." And he was right. There was no need for me to respond with a witty comeback. In reality, acknowledging people like that was a waste of time. For all I knew, I could be arguing with some thirteen-year-old kid who was ranting while his mom made him macaroni and cheese. I had no way of knowing why any of those people were commenting. Things really got bad when I started streaming because people would try to get me riled up so they could see a live reaction. Way too often I would take the bait and respond, but all this ever achieved was a useless back-and-forth exchange that was completely negative and a waste of time.

It wasn't until a year ago that I learned to let it go and not engage. I read all the comments and it's safe to say there are a lot more good ones than bad ones. The good ones are appreciated, but I can't take those to heart either and let any opinion, even if it's good, make me feel a certain way. If I'm on stream and see that the comments are getting really bad, I'll reply and say something like "I see you're not enjoying this, why don't you go check out a stream you do enjoy?"

Getting into those types of arguments online doesn't solve anything. People are going to say what they're going to say.

I've come so far since I first started, and nothing makes that more obvious than going back to look at old videos. I used to do a lot of silly types of videos that didn't seem funny at all when I watched them again. Not only did I not think they were funny, but I seemed less confident in them. That has definitely changed, and after all these years in front of the camera, I couldn't help but become a better public speaker. This is true for the stuff behind the camera as well. Edits that used to take me an hour will now only take ten minutes. I have a much better understanding of how much work certain videos will take, which in turn makes me more efficient and better prepared. More importantly, I have learned what to put my effort into.

Not only have I changed over the years, but so has the platform. At the beginning of *Ghosts* in November 2013, YouTube began implementing specific content ID restrictions. For example, if you put popular music in your video past the time when it's considered Creative Commons, YouTube's content ID will recognize that song and flag your video. This would lead to a strike, and if you got three strikes your channel would get terminated. The problem was that there were no repercussions for using copyrighted music in older videos, yet those videos could still be run through the new system, which was crazy.

So last year some random person who I had never met or had any interaction with at all tried to dig up old videos that he could flag. He would tweet me things like "I hate you," "You're a horrible person and I'm going to take your channel down." I was like okay, whatever. This was just some guy on Twitter who I didn't know, so I didn't think much of it, but then I woke up the next day to see that I had two strikes. He actually went back to find a couple old videos of mine that broke the new guidelines. This was a pretty widespread thing and I know of some YouTubers who actually had their channels terminated temporarily because of it. Luckily that didn't happen to me.

What this guy found in my videos were the tags I put into the

MIDNITE'S FAVORITE VIDEO COLLABORATIONS

I do a lot of stuff with OpTic Jewel. We've known each other for so long and a lot of people view us as a duo. She joined shortly after me and even some of the snipers like Predator were like, "This girl can be huge." She was good at the game, she was the right age, and sure enough, after she posted her video to OpTic Nation, it just blew up. We've created some really cool content and have a lot of fun doing stuff together.

I don't know if this next one is the same thing because it's not technically a video collaboration, but it turned into a huge video. So OpTic Jewel and I were playing league play in *Black Ops 2* when we randomly got matched up against Scumpii. I was live-streaming at the time and it was amazing to watch my views just shoot up so quickly. I have no idea how streaming works, but word gets out fast. When something interesting starts happening, you immediately get more views. That was the case here. Somehow we ended up beating him. I have no idea how. So I asked him if he would mind if I uploaded it. He didn't care and told me to go ahead. I posted the video and it blew up. It's still one of the more popular videos on my channel.

description. Before the new restrictions, it was common for YouTubers to put tags in the videos like *"Call of Duty," "Call of Duty Black Ops 2," "Call of Duty* multiplayer"—just common words that could help your video come up in search results. After the restrictions, you could use these same words, but they had to be in a sentence when describing the video. You couldn't just have random tags in the description. It was basically neglect on my part. I knew that old videos could get flagged, but I figured who's going to go and do that? It was a minor detail, but that's how he caught me.

Now I had to go back and edit the descriptions of all my videos. Thank God that YouTube had a mass edit function, so I didn't have to go through thousands of videos one at a time. If that didn't exist, I'd probably still be editing them now. That was when I really buckled down and put in the time to fix those things because there were people out there actually looking to bring down my channel. I even made a video about the whole thing. While I was going through that, it was great to have somebody like Fwiz in my corner. He worked for YouTube, so he could guide me through that process and vouch for me. Now I know the rules, and as long as I abide by those rules, something like this won't happen again.

24

HOW DID IT GET SO DAMN UGLY?

Scump

The whole being-a-pro-player thing . . . people think it's this glorious lifestyle and great all the time, but there is a lot of stress. We have a ton of fans who are great, but there is that small group of people who just want to see us fail. With YouTube and streaming, I really have to be careful about what I say and do. A lot of people try to talk down to me and get into my personal life. Bad publicity can kill a pro player, so I don't want to react or say something stupid. Those people who don't want to see me succeed will jump right on that kind of stuff. The majority of the fans aren't like that, but it's hard to ignore that one rotten egg. I'm not saying it's a bad lifestyle. I definitely love what I do and wouldn't want to do anything else, but people don't realize there's a lot of pressure on the pro players.

I always dreamed about being a pro, but back in the day there was no YouTube, so I never even imagined video making being a part of any of this. The amount of people watching our videos is mind-blowing to me and it's something that I don't think I'll ever be able to wrap my head around. That's one of the weird things that takes

188 // OPTIC GAMING

some getting used to. Our whole lives are broadcast for anybody to see. We don't have much privacy. We don't get to hide many secrets because people find out about them. When I make a ten-minute video, I'm saying a lot of stuff. The fans who have been watching my videos regularly probably know everything about me. It's something we just have to accept.

I guess it's intrusive, but it's not a big deal for me to sit down and talk about myself. I feel like my subscribers are my friends. They know my tendencies. I'm pushing a video every day, so they hear me talk about what's on my mind, but the place where this really comes out is during the live streams. I like streaming more than YouTube. Streaming is an ongoing thing for hours on end. It includes the highs and lows instead of a quick five-minute clip on YouTube. If I'm having a shitty day, it's obvious.

The tough part of all this is that the fans from opposing teams also know everything about me. Those are some of the people who take the most personal shots that they can. They're hiding behind the keyboard, so they don't see it as being a problem. If I make one mistake, they'll keep picking at that mistake until they run it into the ground. In the end, I just have to block them out. I don't want to get in a position where I'm not posting a video because I'm worried about what the haters are gonna think.

I gotta admit that is has gotten better. People used to be absolute savages on Twitter—not just fans, but players too. So many players were completely reckless and didn't care what they said. This just made those players look horrible. People could take screenshots of what you said and it would come back to haunt you. If you said that kind of crazy stuff today, you'd literally be cooking yourself up and serving yourself up on a plate to get criticized by everyone. That's why all the crap talk has died down. It never completely went away, but players have gotten more professional. And the people that haven't are considered a liability and have difficulty finding sponsors.

My YouTube channel has always been pretty clean, and because of YouTube, I've learned what not to say. When I started out, people would take some of the things I said a completely different way from how I meant them. There were a couple of times where I was just messing around, but some people got all upset. They jumped down my throat. "Stop being an ass. He's not a pro player. Who do you think you are?" In my mind, I'm just messing around. I wasn't being serious. I learned to be careful, and in the back of my head I'm always thinking how a certain comment will come off or be perceived. I still slip up, but some of these things have become second nature, and honestly, a lot of it is just common sense that comes with getting older.

It's hard to watch some of my old videos. The one thing I've noticed is that I used to come off a little cocky. It felt like I thought I was better than everyone else. I may have firmly believed that, and I still firmly believe it, but the way that I was talking made me seem like an ass. I didn't think I was doing anything wrong, but when I'd sit down and rewatch the video, I could see how I might have been out of line, or how my tone of voice made me come off a certain way that I didn't want to be perceived as. I don't talk like that now. In a weird kind of way, I sort of learned more about myself by having other people critique my videos on YouTube.

YO, YO, YO!

My intro was something I just picked up and started saying. There's nothing special about it and there's really no story behind it. It's just what I've always done. It's been the same and hasn't changed, except for those couple weeks when I left OpTic. I'll get to that in a sec, but it was pretty weird cutting OpTic out of my name. "Yo, yo, yo, it's your boy Scumpii." That doesn't really sound right, and I had a hard time saying it because I was so used to saying OpTic Scumpii. When it came to my outro, I got that from my best friend in high school. He'd always say "see ya" and look so goofy doing it, so I kind of adopted that.

In the first couple of videos I made, you could tell that I was shy and not really myself, but it didn't take long before I found my niche. I was posting a video every day back when I started. I'd come home and immediately make a video for the next day so I'd always have them done a day in advance. I got into a routine and never really got out of it. A lot of my content was basically the same. There've always been games that people's channels do better on. *Call of Duty* videos always tend to get the most views on my channel—specifically *Black Ops 2*. That's always been the game people enjoy watching the most. People always saw me as a really good *Call of Duty* player, so that's what I try to focus on when I make videos.

XJawz was a YouTuber I'd watch a lot when I was learning how to do it. The same with TmarTn, who I'm really good friends with now. I'd watch all the big *Call of Duty* YouTubers regularly. They all showed me that it was possible to make different types of videos. I didn't have to do just one thing over and over. I could be versatile. If I did it well, people would enjoy it. Once we moved into the OpTic House, I started doing more vlogs and skits, so my channel just grew from there.

Wait, hang on . . . what were we talking about? See how easy it is to get wrapped up in all this? I started off talking about being a pro player and got caught up in YouTube. That's what happens, and that's kind of what started happening during *Black Ops 2*. It was easy to get so focused on YouTube and streaming because it was so time-consuming. That part of it was fun, but not winning was eating away at the inside of me. It was stressful, but what made this so much easier to deal with was that we were all going through it together at the house. If I was off living by myself, it would be so much more difficult. Even then, we still wanted to win and set out to change things during *Ghosts*.

The first event of the season was MLG Columbus in November 2013. This was right after the game came out. It was the biggest MLG *Call of Duty* event to date. We went into the event thinking we were going to do well, but got completely caught off guard by a couple different teams. Things went downhill. Before we even knew what happened, we got knocked out of the winners' bracket in the first round. We won our next match, but then got upset again by JusTus and finished thirteenth. That was it. We were going home.

It's not like we suddenly became worse players during this time. That's not going to happen. Once you become a pro, it's really hard to fall off and take a step back. I first learned this during *MW2* when I came into my own and hit my stride. The pro mentality is like instinct or riding a bike (which I only learned how to do last year). Regardless of the situation in the game, you know how to handle it. Whenever a new *Call of Duty* comes out, everyone is trying to figure out who is going to be the best this particular season, but all the pro players know that if you're good at one *Call of Duty,* you're going to be good at another. That's just the way it is, but something was wrong because we weren't winning. We weren't even coming close. We just finished thirteenth.

I was getting so stressed out and unhappy that I finally lost it at UMG Philadelphia in January of 2014. I was pissed! After the tournament, I packed up my stuff at the team house and made the twelve-hour drive back to my hometown. I just wanted to get away from there and everyone on the team.

It wasn't just what happened in Philadelphia. Things had been building for a while. It started at the team house. The house was supposed to be for practice, but it turned into a YouTube and Twitch competition to see who could get the most viewers. I think the team house was used the wrong way and this tore us apart. I started noticing a lot of subtle shots on live stream. People would say things that would be very vague, but I could tell they were talking about me. That kept happening and then the fans would get on me about it. I wasn't getting along with Matt and the fact that we lived together created even more friction.

I was approached by EnVyUs. They already had ProoFy and MerK, who I had teamed with before. Their fourth was Goonjar, and Rambo was their coach. It was tempting when they asked me to join and the anger I had toward OpTic at the time kind of pushed me over

THE DARK TIMES

When Seth left, this was the only time I felt hurt by a roster move. It only lasted a couple of weeks, but this whole period was just bad. Just thinking about it hurts my stomach. For the first time in the history of OpTic, the roster was in disarray. We went through a lot of players, and I was worried that it was going to turn into this thing where people didn't want to team with NaDeSHoT.

Everything exploded in Philadelphia. One of NaDeSHoT's flaws was that if Seth made a mistake during the game, he'd be on his ass. You don't do that midgame. You point out the mistake and then discuss it after. Not during the game. Seth got sick of it. They had just lost. Again. That was not the reaction he needed to hear at the time from NaDeSHoT. It reached a point where Seth said, "I either need my own team or I'm going to EnVy."

NaDeSHoT came to me and said, "Seth is the best player, we can't let him go. I'll step down." That right there was all I needed to hear, and it's one of the reasons why I'll always have his back. He was willing to sacrifice himself for the good of the team. I was immediately like, "No. Fuck him. You're staying. He's going. We'll figure it out." NaDeSHoT was super out of line in Philadelphia, so I do understand Seth's decision to leave, but it was the way he did it that pissed me off. He went behind my back and started talking to a different team. That was just not good.

It felt like the world was crashing down. That was such a negative time in my life. I hate talking about it. I remember sitting there and thinking, *What the fuck are we going to do?* Players were under contract at this point, so we couldn't go and pick up other players because they couldn't leave. We had almost no control over our situation. I learned then never to let a contract expire because it leaves you helpless. The fans hated it just as much because they saw us as the one stable team, and if we were falling apart, how long before everything falls apart? How long before teams start to die? It was a bad time for OpTic and *Call of Duty*.

—H3CZ

the edge. I left OpTic for EnVyUs. So now there would be no "OpTic" in front of Scumpii.

I made a rash decision without thinking things through. All I wanted was to start winning again. Placing thirteenth in back-to-back tournaments was not okay to me. We had never experienced failure like this before and people were pointing fingers at each other. Shit hit the fan and I did not react well. Look, I know I messed up and I will tell everybody that now. I was a kid back then and it was a childish thing for me to do.

PART 6

ADVANCED WARFARE

25

ROCK BOTTOM

NaDeSHoT

We could have written this whole damn book about *Call of Duty: Ghosts* alone. That 2014 season was like a soap opera. It was a crazy time to be a part of OpTic and a fan of OpTic. It started with BigTymeR retiring and then everything kind of blew up at UMG Philadelphia.

I was pretty hard on Scump because I think he made a lot of bad decisions in that tournament, but I also think he was just sick of me being such a vocal player. He's always been the best player, but sometimes he can do some real stupid shit. After we got into it, he was going around telling people how much he hated me and didn't want to be on the team. He was sending nasty texts and we were going back and forth. We finally stopped talking to each other. When he joined EnVyUs I was happy that I didn't have to deal with him. It was a relief to know that we wouldn't be arguing anymore.

I don't think the competition at the house had anything to do with him leaving. I know Scump always refers to the house as being a living hell, but I think that was more him being immature. I was immature in a sense too when I would give in to these arguments, but it wasn't because of the house. He could have made things easier on himself by going out and buying furniture. I make fun of him for that all the time. I think a fight like this needed to happen because of how much we argued.

We picked up MBoZe and we were playing well. Scump's team wasn't doing well at all, so I guess he hit up Hector asking to come back. From a player standpoint I wanted Scump back because he was so good, but after everything that happened, I didn't want to play with him again. I also knew exactly why he was coming back too. His viewership was down and he needed that OpTic push to get his numbers up. He will never admit it, but I talk shit to him about it all the time. At the end of the day, we decided to bring him back on the team. I put all the personal stuff aside because I knew he made us better. We're good friends now that there isn't any pressure on us and we're not competing against each other.

Scump was back and we rounded out our new roster with Clayster and ProoFy, but we still couldn't get it together. We were scrimming on and off. We were really inconsistent. Going into X Games, I didn't expect to win. I had no idea what was going to happen, but never in a million years did I think I would leave Austin with a gold medal— not the way we were playing. That whole experience was just mind-blowing for me. Winning that gold medal meant so much because it was the first MLG event that I ever won. That had been a dream of mine since I used to watch *Halo 2* tournaments on USA.

X Games was hands down the best I ever played. I was putting up numbers in Search and Destroy and absolutely going off. I was on another level at that event and I have no explanation for any of it. A lot of *Call of Duty* is just timing and luck in a sense. You can understand the game down to every single situation, but if you don't get lucky and have good timing, things aren't going to work in your favor. I took a lot of risks in those matches and every single time it just worked out. I should have gone to the damn casino that night because that's how lucky I was getting. Every decision I made worked. Every call I made worked. It might have been the pressure or the stage, but I just got lucky. I felt like Neo in *The Matrix*. I knew what everybody else was going to do and what was going to happen. We carried this momentum into the next event in Anaheim and should have won that tournament too, but we came in second to CompLexity.

June was the only bright spot of that year, but even though we played well, I could tell something was definitely off. I think I have a really good eye for what's going to make a team win. *Call of Duty* is a game where if something isn't working, it probably never will. If your team doesn't click in the first three or four weeks, there isn't much you can do to fix it.

We needed a change. Clayster wasn't doing very well. He was a great player, but *Ghosts* wasn't his title, so he was struggling. ProoFy would have games where he would go absolutely off. He could have a monster game, but then he'd be inconsistent. And I'm really good friends with ProoFy. We've been good friends since 2008. He's one of the nicest guys you'll ever meet and just a genuinely good person, but I knew it was necessary to replace him and Clayster. This is what's so tough about competitive *Call of Duty*. You make these friendships, but if something's not working you have to change it right away because all the fans want is for you to win.

What made this decision even harder was that the team was scheduled to go to the Red Bull eSports camp for the entire month of September. The competitive team moved into a house in Los Angeles. We would stream from the Red Bull studios and play our online matches, but the real reason we were there was to improve our chemistry and play better as a team. It was physical and mental. Everything we did was health-oriented. We did yoga twice a week and learned how to improve our diets. We did all this physical training to get us in better overall shape. They put these helmets on us so they could do EEG testing. The point was to read our brain activity to look for patterns when we play. We even spoke with a sports psychologist and did these team-building exercises, but just because we were doing this Red Bull camp didn't mean we could stop our own business. It was such a weird time because they were making this whole documentary about our experience, but we were thinking about making roster changes.

I don't want to sound like I was scheming, but I told Scump, "We need to make a change. *Advanced Warfare* is coming out soon. It will be a brand-new season. We need to find some new teammates." Scump is the best player in the game, but one of the most frustrating things for me is that sometimes he can be an airhead. He knows it. I make fun of him all the time for it. So when I asked him about these roster moves, he didn't have an opinion. That drove me crazy because I'm the kind of person who would sit there and think about everything from every possible angle. I'd dissect certain attributes of a player and try to figure out how that player might help our chances to win, but Scump didn't care about any of that. He just wanted to play. He told me, "Do whatever you think is best." I wanted so badly for him to have an opinion about this, because I didn't have anybody else to talk to about it.

So this became my decision. I told Hector that I thought we should go after Crimsix for *Advanced Warfare*. Crimsix was one of the best players and one of the smartest players. He started his playing career during *Modern Warfare 2* and dabbled in *Halo* before coming back to *Call of Duty* and being incredibly consistent during *Black Ops 2*. He had won so many championships by that point that it was difficult to keep track of them all. I needed a player like him by my side to help make decisions and lead the team. So after our last event in Columbus, we made the decision to approach Crimsix. Scump and I pulled him aside right there at the venue and talked to him about joining OpTic even though he was still under contract with EG.

Originally it was going to be me, Scump, Crimsix, and Clayster, but Crimsix said that he'd rather team with FormaL than Clayster. I agreed. Clayster and I had a lot of arguments and we didn't always get along. FormaL was another *Halo* player who quickly made a name for himself in *Call of Duty*. I was all for it. So now it would be Scump, Crimsix, FormaL, and me. That would be the team for *Advanced*

Warfare and I knew it would work. So we went ahead and made the change, but all the fans were so pissed at us for dropping Clayster and ProoFy. People acted like we'd just committed murder. It was a tough time to be a member of OpTic Gaming, but it had to be done. And it worked. I'll let our tournament results speak for that decision.

We got off to a good start. One of my key strengths is that I'm always one of the best players at the beginning of the season. I learn the game really fast and that's something I pride myself on. Everything was going great at the beginning of 2015. I loved *Advanced Warfare* at first. I loved how different the game was and how fast it was. Everything is more fun when you're winning and we were this unstoppable team for a couple of months. As time went on and players got better I think the game got too fast for me. I'm a strategic player and a very aggressive player, but that game just allowed everyone else to be aggressive and it exposed every weakness I had. I'm a smart player, but I don't have the best gun skills in the world. I can shoot and hold my own, but if I get into a one-on-one confrontation, it's probably fifty-fifty. That's tough for me.

As the season progressed, it felt like I was getting worse and everyone else was getting better. Everything came to a head in March during *Call of Duty* Champs in Los Angeles when we finished an extremely disappointing seventh. This wasn't the worst I've ever placed, but I would call this my worst tournament experience. Everybody was expecting us to win that event and nothing went our way. Nothing worked. There I was sitting in the booth next to the three best players in the game, and they were so incredibly pissed that we weren't winning. Nothing clicked. We were panicking. It was awful.

As the seconds started to tick down in that final match, I already knew that this would be my last event. There was no way I could stay on this team after playing this badly. My teammates would never say that they wanted to get rid of me, but I knew for a fact that they didn't want me on the team. I had to leave and that was the worst feeling.

I was 100 percent burned out. I admit that. I had to make videos and stream every day, and I had done this for three years by that point. The grind catches up to you, but it wasn't only about the grind. I was so incredibly sick of being the scapegoat. Even if I wasn't the reason we lost, I was the one they pointed the finger at. That was just the reputation I had developed over the years. FormaL, Crimsix, and Scump were considered the best players in the world, and since I was not at their level, I was the one everyone blamed when things went wrong.

After Champs, I was getting hate tweets all day. All my chat and YouTube comments were just hate and I was so sick of reading it. I was so done with being that player on that team. I didn't need to hear all the negativity. It got to me. I did a pretty good job of trying not to let it bother me for a very long time, but there are some days when you doubt yourself or lack confidence. The nasty comments wear you down and get to your psyche. People tell me to ignore them, and I do have some really thick skin, but even to this day I still have people making jokes about my dead mother. That's not something you get taught how to deal with in school. You just have to figure out how to process that kind of stuff in your own way.

I made the decision to officially take a break from competitive *Call of Duty*. I knew that if the team had someone better than me, they could win every single event.

26

LOSING A LEGEND

H3CZ

NaDeSHoT's decision to retire didn't come as a surprise to me. The guy's one of my best friends. We talk every day, and this was something we'd been discussing for a while. He had been saying things like "Man, I can retire right now and focus on my You-Tube career." He was talented, but he tends to get into his own head sometimes. I could see him stressing himself out and getting negative, so I was going to do what any good friend would do and support whatever made him the happiest.

NaDeSHoT has always been his own harshest critic. He's the guy who will always take the blame. He's brutally honest with himself and when he's not doing well he will own up to it. At the end of the day, all that matters is what he thinks of himself. A lot of people put that loss at the *Call of Duty* Championships on his shoulders, and even though he didn't play well, it wasn't entirely his fault.

He stepped away because it was time for the next chapter in his life. He's very good at assessing a situation from a third-person standpoint and seeing the bigger picture. He knew that once his playing career was over, he'd have to go to work, and work for him was the entertainment side of gaming. Since he's left competitive *Call of Duty*, he's been able to free himself from a lot of stress. He's no longer judged as a player. I don't know if he's created as much content as he intended to create when he first made the decision to quit the team. That's a question you have to ask him, but as long as the dude's happy, I'm glad that he did what he did.

As much as I like to give NaDeSHoT credit as a player, in the eyes of the average fan he was never all-star caliber. Still, he always had his moments of brilliance while competing. Who knows? *Advance Warfare* could have been the game that he got better at as the season progressed. At times it just felt like he understood the game better than anyone else. He was the guy that got dirty and disrupted the other team so much that it caused them to lose. I like to think the team would have succeeded and that Seth, Crimsix, and FormaL would have known how to win with him in the lineup.

I'd be lying if I said that it didn't cross my mind that NaDeSHoT's absence would impact the popularity of the team and the sport in general, but I wasn't too worried. We've been through that before. We've had big personalities leave the team, and I knew that we'd lose a small fraction of the fan base. NaDeSHoT was such a big personality that some of his followers wouldn't continue to tune in without him on the team. That was unavoidable, but we weren't losing him altogether. He would still be a part of the team as a personality, and that's what he was best at.

NaDeSHoT was the guy who was pushing boundaries and helped set the example for what an eSports athlete should be. He was making a play for something bigger and that has always been the goal. He was the first eSports player to hit five hundred thousand subscribers. At the beginning of 2015, he reached one million, and last fall he passed two million. I can only imagine how many he has at the time you're reading this.

In spite of his popularity, he was now off the competitive team and we had to find a replacement to fill in for the remainder of the

Advanced Warfare season. Knowing the talent of our core three, Seth, Crimsix, and FormaL, I wasn't at all worried that we could pick up a fourth and continue to win. I honestly believed that those three could play with anyone. Luckily, we already had NaDeSHoT's replacement lined up and he played on OpTic Nation, which made for a smooth transition. Damon "Karma" Barlow was going to be the player to fill some very big shoes.

Not only was Karma the best player in the game during *Black Ops 2,* but he had played with Crimsix on Evil Geniuses the previous year, so they had that chemistry. In fact we picked up Karma and Crimsix as a package deal when EG broke up. I wanted to put Crimsix on OpTic Gaming, but I also wanted to make OpTic Nation a top-tier team after they started competing again as our second team during *Ghosts.*

The beauty of building up OpTic Nation was that we had unintentionally prepared ourselves for this exact situation without even realizing it. We had a number of different players who could fill in on OpTic Gaming in the event of an unexpected roster change. It wasn't like we were sabotaging Nation either, because they were having their own chemistry issues before we moved Karma. It was now just a matter of him meshing with the other three. Damon has always been that utility player, so he could carry out any assignment and do it well. You only worry about chemistry when you don't have a team of talented players and that was not the case here. This put my mind at ease and I knew we would continue to have a successful year.

27

THERE'S NOTHING BETTER THAN WINNING

Scump

I personally don't think NaDeSHoT was holding us back. In his head, I think that he felt like he wasn't at the level of the other three players on his team. That gave him anxiety. He blamed himself, so he skipped. That's what I would guess, but I really have no idea. I never talked to him about it.

Going into Champs, we were the best team on paper. This is the one tournament that all the pros want to win every year. It's the one with the best accommodations and it's a million-dollar tournament, so it's the one with the most money on the line. Usually the *Call of Duty* Championships is my best tournament of the year, but this time around it was just rough. We lost to Denial, who was the second-best team in the game, so that was understandable. Then we lost to FaZe. This was before they hit their stride, so it was a huge letdown. We choked at the worst possible time. I really have no idea what happened. Maybe people were nervous. I couldn't tell you. Nobody can.

Luckily I didn't have to take that long flight back to Chicago.

That would have been awful. I was with my girlfriend and she lived in nearby Orange County, so that's where I was going to stay for the next couple of months. Still, without even seeing Matt, I could tell that seventh-place finish was bothering him. Things were awkward between all of us and everyone was so pissed off. NaDeSHoT then told us all at once: "All right, I'm not happy and I think you guys can get a better teammate. I'm not good enough to be on this team and I know it." It was kind of depressing. Then he just left the team.

Matt always talked about taking a break, but I never thought he would just straight-up, cold-turkey retire after Champs. It was never mentioned in a way that made it seem immediate. Like he didn't say, "If we lose this tournament I'm gone." Nobody on the team expected it, and the fan reaction was insane. NaDeSHoT was the face of *Call of Duty,* so it was a big surprise when he retired. Even to this day, people still ask him to come back. We'll see what he ends up doing, but it was definitely an earth-shattering decision on his part.

With NaDeSHoT gone, I took over as the captain of the competitive team, but the idea of not playing with Matt was weird. Just because I wanted to punch him in the mouth sometimes didn't mean I didn't like him. He got under my skin, definitely, but in spite of all that, he was like a brother to me and that was the type of relationship we had. We weren't always at each other's throat, but when we were, we were ready to throw hands.

As soon as we picked up Karma I just wanted to start practicing so we could start winning again, if for no other reason than to prove that we were still the best. It was definitely a stressful period, but being able to pick up a player like Karma put our minds at ease. He was the obvious choice from the very beginning. He's always been a top player and he was a great fit for *Advanced Warfare* in particular because he was just so consistent with every gun. He was also a good guy, which always helps when you need somebody to jump onto the roster midseason. It's not always about raw skill.

Everyone was excited for the European LANs in May. We'd be playing one weekend in Paris at ESWC and then the next weekend in

London at Gfinity, but Karma, who was from Canada, was still getting his American citizenship in order, so he couldn't leave the country. This wasn't a big deal. We were focused on X Games in June and we knew Karma would be the guy we'd be playing with when we got back from Europe. It was a minor speed bump.

FaZe wasn't going to Europe and the guys on our team were already really good friends with Enable from FaZe. I had known him since the *Black Ops 1* days. More importantly, he fit our team very well. He was a good AR player, which was what we needed. He used to play *Halo,* which meant that he communicated well, and that alone made him a good teammate. So we asked FaZe if we could take one of their players for the two events in Europe. They said yes, so we scooped him up.

This trip to Europe turned out to be a great experience all around. I was super excited because this would be my first time in Paris and at an ESWC event. This tournament was just insane. It was super hot on that main stage during the grand final and I was dripping sweat, but I have to say that this was the greatest crowd I ever played in front of in my life. The size, noise, and passion was much different from anything we were used to. It took me like two days to come down from the high of winning that tournament. They host that tournament every year, but this was the first year that we went. I guess it's always insane because it's usually held during Paris Games Week, which is a convention, so everybody is there at the *Call of Duty* event for the finals. I'm hoping that it will be an annual stop for us from here on out. From there it was on to Gfinity for another great tournament and we took back-to-back first-place finishes.

We flew back home, but couldn't get too comfortable because we had UMG California the following week. We also had Karma back. Enable did a great job filling in over in Europe. He helped us win both tournaments, but now it was on to California, where we would play with our new roster for the first time. We knew we just had to keep doing the same thing. Karma and Enable were similar players and played the same role, so that transition was easy. It was more about

GOING ABROAD

The ESWC tournament was an eye-opener for what could be here in the United States. The *Call of Duty* fans there were not just fans of OpTic. They were fans of everyone. Here in the United States you have this very loud group of Green Wall supporters, while there are other teams that don't really have any fans. In Paris, the crowd was so into the tournament that they would cheer regardless of who made a good play. As a fan, I find myself doing this too. At this point, I can appreciate the game for what it is. I'm a fan of the Chicago Bears, but I can watch highlights on ESPN and appreciate seeing amazing plays no matter what the team. That's kind of what was happening in Paris and it's the kind of reaction we would love to start seeing here in the United States. I think it's possible too.

The tournament was great and the fans were phenomenal, but the hotel was a nightmare. I was supposed to be with the team in Europe for the full two weeks, but unfortunately I couldn't make the trip to London. The heater in my Paris hotel room wasn't working, so it was freezing every night and it was raining to top it off. Even at night I would sleep with a sweater on and grab the extra covers, but I couldn't get away from it. Everything was so damp that I could just feel a cold chill. By that Sunday, I knew that if I traveled with the team to London, it would be miserable for me and everyone else because I would have been awful to be around. I decided to come home early, and sure enough, the second I landed in the United States, I was already sick.

That Paris hotel was bad, but the London hotels are by far the worst. I'm not lying when I say that the closet in my master bedroom is bigger than the room I stayed in last time I was in London. It was an eight-by-ten square box with a single bed that touched the wall. I'm surprised they could even fit a bed in there. It was just bad. It's usually like this anytime we go to Gfinity, which is another great tournament, by the way. They put us in the hotel that is closest to the venue, and nowadays Gfinity has

their own arena in a theater. We can rely on the fact that we will probably be staying at the same hotel because of its proximity to the venue.
The same is true when traveling in the United States, but even a Motel 6
has bigger rooms than the hotels in London, which appears to be a very
space-conscious city.

—H3CZ

getting used to his communication because Karma had a couple different tendencies, but overall it wasn't much different.

After winning with Enable two weekends in a row, we found ourselves playing against him and FaZe the very next weekend. We got
off to a superslow start and were making a ton of mistakes. We lost
that first match to FaZe, but would get a second chance against them
in the grand final. We had teamed with Enable and he knew what we
did, but even that wasn't really a disadvantage. Strategies change, and
the only tendencies he could possibly pick up on from playing with us
and use effectively would be in something like Search and Destroy,
where he could be like, "He's going to go here this round, so look
there and pre-aim it." If I don't go there and they don't get that kill,
then there is really no benefit to having played with us at all. That
works both ways. He may know my tendencies, but I can play mind
games with him by completely switching up those tendencies so he
won't know what's going on. Sometimes it can help, but sometimes it
can backfire when you think you know the other team members so
well and they end up doing something you never saw coming. So like
I said, it didn't really matter.

The problem was that we weren't playing well. We were slow out
of the gate again during the final, so during a break, I pulled the team
outside before the next series. I told them it felt like we were trying to
force a win. We were making stupid mistakes and putting pressure on

ourselves. I tried to get everyone to calm down before we went inside. "Just play and have fun. If we lose, we lose." That's what we did, and an hour later we had won our third tournament in a row.

May 2015 we were on fire. I don't know if I'd ever won three tournaments in a year before, and here we'd just won three tournaments in the same month. Actually, we just won three tournaments in three weekends in three different countries. How about that? I was so hyped and so proud of everyone. This was huge for us. In spite of the roster change and the poor placing at Champs, we were still okay. We knew we would be, but it was reassurance. Now things were clicking. What's great about competitive *Call of Duty* is that once your team finds chemistry, it's really hard to lose it.

We couldn't have hit our stride at a better time because X Games was coming up again in June. This was the tournament everyone on the team had been getting hyped for ever since that loss at Champs. We won it the previous year, but that didn't make it any less exciting. If anything, it made it more exciting because we knew how big this was and what a huge win it would be for the team. I wanted another gold medal. How many times do you get that chance? I personally prepared like a madman. Unlike the previous year, the team was pulling ten-hour days practicing for this event. We were trying to work on our weak maps, and we were just hoping to ride that momentum we built from those previous tournament wins. We. Would. Not. Lose.

We were headed back to Austin, just like the previous year for *Ghosts,* but now they put us in a more crowded area. There were a lot of different events going on around us, which was cool. Motocross racing was nearby, and Saturday there were like five hundred people outside the gaming tent, but when we were in the tent we were just focused on the game. None of the other sports mattered. We were only there to win the event.

There were still eight teams (and we were the number one seed), but it would be a straight-up double-elimination best-of-seven bracket. That meant best of seven matches the whole way through, and that favored us. Remember how I said those Friday tournament matches

28

OPTIC'S BEST YEAR EVER?

H3CZ

think this OpTic Gaming roster was the best one competitive *Call of Duty* had ever seen. Somehow we managed to go through the entire year with only one roster change. NaDeSHoT's decision to step down didn't have an impact on the popularity of the professional team or its success from a business standpoint. We were still able to sell the same amount of sponsorships. Karma got off to a slow start, but he came on strong. This group of guys could get pretty far on pure talent alone, but the further we got into the season, the more everyone began to catch up, and that's when chemistry came into play.

Never did I realize how important chemistry was until I saw OpTic Nation struggle during the *Advanced Warfare* season in 2015. Looking at it from a third-person perspective, and not taking the personality aspect into account, the OpTic Nation team had an up-and-down season. They were very inconsistent. They placed really well at Champs. They finished fourth, which was better than OpTic Gaming. Unfortunately, there wasn't that one stable player the team could rely

H3CZ'S OPTIC GAMING DREAM TEAM

The competitive team I put together for this list should look familiar because it's the team we have now and by far the best team we've ever had for any season. If the goal is to put together an all-time great OpTic team to go out and compete, these are the guys I would pick. I wouldn't pick any player from any other era, and I say that with absolute certainty. If I were to put my money on any one team, it would be this one.

1. Scump
2. Crimsix
3. FormaL
4. Karma

on in the clutch. If you look at all the good teams, they usually have one or two guys on their roster who hold everything together. This past *Advanced Warfare* season was a bit of a letdown, but that's just a part of the game.

We need someone to emerge as the leader on Nation, the guy the others can rely on and go to for instruction or turn to when they need to dig themselves out of a hole. Next season will be a different game, so just because somebody didn't do well in a very fast, jet-pack-heavy game like *Advanced Warfare* doesn't mean they won't be able to do well in a game that's a little slower and closer to traditional *Call of Duty*. We'll find out how they do during *Black Ops 3*.

Whether it's watching OpTic Gaming or OpTic Nation, I'm always more of a spectator at events. I'm there for moral support. I don't coach them or anything. They're left to fend for themselves when it comes to making sure they have enough food. That's all on them. Besides, I don't think there's anything that I can tell the players that they don't already know. I also take a lot of meetings at events. I try to catch up with other owners and speak to any potential sponsors who show up and want to see what *Call of Duty* looks like from the ground floor.

There are some situations at events when I have to mediate between the players and the league. In the middle of a game, it isn't uncommon for a player on either team to get disconnected. This usually turns into an argument. If one team is winning, they'll want to pick up from where they were, but if that team is losing, they could claim they were about to mount a comeback and want to start over. That's when the players start arguing with the league and it's during this type of situation that I try to step in. Even if we were the team that was winning at the time, and the other team wants to start over, it's usually best to start over in these situations. That way you win outright and people won't blame a win on what they feel was an unfair decision.

There are other bigger-picture scenarios that I have to look out for as a team owner during events. I want to make sure that the league isn't showing favoritism to my team because they're the popular fan favorite. The opposite is true as well and I have to be on the lookout for any time when it seems like the league is trying to make an example out of OpTic because we are the biggest. I try to keep everything as fair as possible because that's the only way that true competition can be attained.

I want to be close by during matches in case something happens, but I don't sit in the stands ever. Sometimes I'll sit down in the stands and start talking with the fans and then look up to see that the team lost the first game. Immediately I get up. "It's my fault. I'm leaving." The fans laugh. They know why I'm leaving. So I go watch the game in the VIP room or go back to my room if I can. During the first X Games, I was kind of forced to watch the match from the stands. The hotel was so far away from the venue and it was so sunny that I couldn't see anything on my iPhone. Luckily the team won, but the entire time I was nervous. Just being there added to my own personal stress. I don't know, but I'm very superstitious. I feel like my presence there jinxes the team. If it ever seems like the team is going to lose, I make it a point to be there. It's easy to show up for the success, but it's after the failures when I really need to be there so I can tell them to keep their heads up.

During this past *Advanced Warfare* season, I made another conscious effort to produce more content on my own channel. I even shot a couple behind-the-scenes videos while we were at tournaments. During *Black Ops 1,* I took a step back from making content to focus more on growing OpTic. I would still make videos, but I wasn't uploading daily and that's what it takes to be a YouTuber. If you're not already a huge presence, you have to upload consistently in order to keep up with the times and generate an interest from your audience so they keep coming back. You want them engaged so even if they can't watch your content on a daily basis, they're going to catch up with what you've done at the end of the week when they do have time.

I constantly go through this mental struggle where I wonder where I'd be if I committed more time to my own channel. I started out as an entertainer. I know how to make videos. I know what people want to watch. I know how to be creative. I know I could have become a very good YouTuber, so I always fall back on the what-ifs. My channel is at 630,000 subscribers right now and I realize that hitting that one-million mark is within reach. That is something I can go for, but every day is a struggle to balance all of my responsibilities. I give myself a lot of credit for being able to manage my time and stay on top of it all, but the YouTube thing is not something I want to put out there simply because. I have so much respect for the YouTube grind that I don't want to toss stuff up there just to see if it sticks. I want to take the time to really make the video I want and to make sure that it's a good video. That is the struggle, but it is something I want to do more of.

The time when it's most difficult to be consistent is on the road. The scene is growing and this past year OpTic Gaming went to more tournaments in one year than ever before. We've gotten used to life on the road. I carry my laptop everywhere I go so I can keep in contact while also dealing with any business that might come in. We're lucky enough to be in a situation as a company where we have professionals in our corner to make sure that no business slips through the cracks. The only thing that we may fall behind on are the videos players post on their individual channels. They're supposed to make sure that they have videos ready to go up while they're away. That way there is no disconnect and they can still keep in touch with the fans throughout the weekend.

We ran into a problem last fall with "OpTic Owns October." You may have heard, but my plan was for one member of OpTic to post a vlog on the OpTic Nation channel every day during the month of October. Simple, right? Well, it didn't quite work out that way. We came close, and I think we would have pulled it off if it weren't for bad Internet connections at the hotels. It's a pain because even if you pay the extra twenty dollars a night to upgrade to the top-of-the-line Internet, you're still not going to be in a place that's reliable enough for you to upload videos to YouTube on a consistent basis. Some hotels are better than others, and some locations are better than others, but at the end of the day you're left at the mercy of that connection to post your videos.

We made it to day seventeen of "OpTic Owns October" before we dropped the ball and couldn't continue making daily posts. This was a spur-of-the-moment thing. Nobody out there was doing anything like this, so I figured we'd give it a shot. It's a good way to keep our players and our fan base on their toes. Little things like this can help shake up what we do. We'll try it again, and knowing what we know now, we will be able to pull it off because those videos will be made ahead of time. I knew these types of problems could occur, but we didn't prepare as well as I would have liked. Don't worry, we'll try again soon and get it done.

Back in October, my mind was on other things. The Green Wall was in the midst of the most dominant season in *Call of Duty* history all while playing one of the most polarizing games the sport had ever seen. Players either loved it or hated it, and not everybody who was successful at other games could compete when it came to *Advanced Warfare*. This wasn't a traditional *Call of Duty* game. *Advanced Warfare* was one that required pure skill and reaction time.

29

I LOVED *ADVANCED WARFARE*

Scump

AW was a very different game with a totally different feel. I think Sledgehammer Games did a great job and took a big risk with this one, but it all worked out. I really liked the movements and being able to double jump and zoom around the map. You gotta hit a lot of buttons. It requires a good amount of skill and you have to work much harder on the sticks, but it's the challenge that makes it fun for me. It did take some getting used to. Even I didn't know what to think of the exosuits at first. It was foreign to me, so I had no idea what was going on, but after learning to play with them, I enjoyed it. I'm probably the wrong person to ask about this stuff because I'm a *Call of Duty* freak.

Some people were scared that *AW* would change *Call of Duty*, but I think it improved the game. It had a new element we needed, but what's so funny about *AW* is that some people absolutely hated the game and were just waiting for the next *Call of Duty* to come out. The reason why those people hated it, in my personal opinion, was because it was just too much. If you didn't have a Scuf controller, it was very

222 // OPTIC GAMING

hard to compete. This is probably why viewership was down this past season. It's a fast game, which makes it hard to follow.

If you're one of the people who hate the game, no need to fear. The game changes every year, so we could get a good game one year, and then the next game may be bad for competitive, but good for pubs. Every year the players have to completely relearn the game. Other games like *Counter-Strike* are basically the same game, but the movement and feel within each *Call of Duty* game changes every year. Usually I can tell right away if I like a game, and that was the case with *AW,* but it's not always like that. Sometimes there are patches in the middle of the game that completely change its look and feel. That happened with *Ghosts.* I thought that game was incredible at the beginning when everybody was using the MTAR, but they patched the game completely and everybody sort of stopped liking it because the Vector became the main gun. That made it much campier. Nobody ran around as much. The developer was looking at it from a casual

SCUMP'S GUN SHOW

Sometimes all it takes is one gun for me to fall in love with a game. Every *Call of Duty* title has those two guns that usually stand out. The ACRs from *MW2* and *MW3* are at the top of my list and probably my favorite guns of all time. The PP90 from *MW3* is also on the list, as is the UMP from *Modern Warfare 2.* I also like the FAMAS from *Black Ops 1.* Some games just have better guns because of how the game is made, and in *MW3* all the guns were really enjoyable. I can go on and on because there are so many different guns out there. Something interesting about *Black Ops 3* that they're implementing is the pick and ban system so teams can ban certain guns and attachments before the match even starts. That's really cool for *Call of Duty* because it will make the guns being used much more diverse. I don't know about you, but I'm excited.

point of view and not from a competitive one. If people don't like a certain thing, the gaming company will change it and the competitive community sort of has to deal with it.

The other reason why I loved *AW* so much was because we were the best team in the game. The thirteenth-place finishes from *Ghosts* were no more. Even the third-place finishes from *Black Ops 2*. Gone. I hadn't had a competitive year like this since *Modern Warfare 3*, but the scene back then wasn't close to being like it was during *AW*, so this just felt so much bigger. We were on fire, and now people were just expecting OpTic Gaming to win every single tournament. I enjoyed that. Your boy just thrives under the pressure even though those might be unrealistic expectations. I mean, we just won four tournaments in a row and people didn't hesitate to talk shit when we finished second. Maybe we can get a little bit of slack?

Finishing second was bad enough, but the thing that really started to bother me was that every time we finished second, the team we lost to in the finals was FaZe. During *AW*, we lost to them four times, but I'm not going to count that first tournament of the year in Columbus because our team was new and this wasn't the same FaZe squad that emerged at the end of the year. But there was a period right before Champs where we just couldn't beat FaZe. It turned into a pretty heated rivalry. The matches were intense, but unlike what most people think, OpTic and FaZe didn't hate each other. We were good friends—they had two of our former teammates in Clayster and Enable.

After we won at X Games, FaZe came right back and won two tournaments in a row—UMG Dallas and Gfinity. We had another chance to redeem ourselves at UMG D.C. in September, but things didn't get off to a good start. I'm not even talking about the tournament. I'm talking about the airport. September 3, 2015, was the day from hell; by far the worst travel day I've ever had.

So we got to the airport, went through security, and then learned that our flight was canceled. We couldn't get another flight until nine P.M. We left the airport, killed some time, and then came

224 // OPTIC GAMING

back for our flight. We got to D.C. only to learn that our bags were on a different flight that went to a completely different airport. We couldn't even get them that night because the airport was closed. We had to go back in the morning. Needless to say, things weren't off to a good start.

What I remember most from this tournament aren't the matches. Well, I do, but that's not what I want to talk about right now. What I want to talk about is what happened outside the venue. I was with some of the guys and we saw this homeless guy strolling the streets. He walked right up to us and told us this crazy joke, and then he gave us each a penny. I looked at it as good juju. He was a nice guy. He came up to us and gave us something. He was expecting us to give him money, but we didn't have any, so that didn't happen. He told us to keep the pennies anyway.

When we went inside, I took that penny and put it on my Xbox. We won that match and we won that tournament, so I looked at that penny as a good-luck charm and have been putting it on my Xbox ever since. And I'm not superstitious at all. I don't have any pregame rituals or anything like that, but I am big on karma—the universal balance and not my teammate. It would have been bad karma for me to throw out that penny. That's kind of the same reason why I don't talk trash to any other pro players. Even if it's joking, I don't want to say anything bad because I'm sure it will come around to bite me. I know it's weird, but I really believe it.

Sorry to say that the penny didn't help a few weeks later at the MLG Season 3 Playoffs in Columbus. We lost to FaZe again, and again we choked. FaZe was a hard team for us to finish off. Maybe their play style countered ours very well. I really don't know. It was weird, but I never thought that we wouldn't pull through and get the best of them eventually. We had some kind of mental block, but when we were on our game, we were the better team. If you look at our five events leading up to the final tournament of the year in New Orleans, we only lost to FaZe four times and Epsilon once, whereas

FaZe lost to a whole bunch of teams. Their record wasn't nearly as good. Even though we were having the better season, if we lost to them again during the last tournament of the year, that's what everyone would remember.

The stage was set for the MLG World Finals in New Orleans at the end of October 2015; $100,000 was on the line. In the weeks leading up to that tournament, we had been on a pretty ridiculous practice schedule compared to what we usually do.

This event was epic. MLG used to throw tournaments like this for *Halo* and called it their National Event. They would throw four regular MLG events throughout the season and then their National Event at the end of the year would be for $100,000 for first place. They had never done anything like that for *Call of Duty,* so this was their attempt to get back to their roots in a way. Most of the MLG events leading up to Worlds were geared more toward the online viewer. This one was more for the live spectator. So instead of a couple hundred people inside an arena like the one in Columbus, there were a couple thousand in a convention center.

To win, we would have to play four pool-play matches and four bracket matches. TK was the team in our pool who I was looking out for, but the team that gave us the most trouble in the entire tournament was the first team we played on Friday—a European team called Infused. They had a couple players I hadn't seen before, but props to them. As we've been known to do, we were a little slow out of the gate and found ourselves down 0–2 early. One of the things that's so stressful about tournaments like this is that you can lose twice right off the bat and you're out. That's what happened to us at Champs and we did not want to start off pool play with a loss here.

I wasn't nervous. I had so much confidence in this team and I knew we were going to win. Infused caught us completely off guard. We didn't expect to drop a map to them. We had to step up and play harder. Slowly that's what we did and we pulled ahead. There isn't that one moment where we flip a switch and everything changes. With us, it's more about settling in and getting comfortable, so it's a gradual thing.

Playing on Friday is so much different from playing on Sunday when you're on the big stage and competing against the top teams in the game. It's Sunday. We know it's the last game of the tournament and we're so much closer to that trophy. Fridays just don't feel as serious and a lot of people don't take them seriously. We have to psych ourselves up and it seems to take a little while before we get into that tournament mode. For me, I just try to take it map by map and not get ahead of myself or start thinking about the next map. Once we beat Infused, we just kept winning all the way to Sunday.

GLASSES OR CONTACTS?

This is such a mental thing for me. Do I play in glasses or do I play in contacts? No matter what I do, the day I switch is always bad for me. Back at the first X Games for *Ghosts,* we were playing in the semifinals against EG and I was wearing contacts when I had the worst map of my entire season because one of my contacts had been completely messing with my eye. Anytime I tried to look up at my minimap, it felt like there was a bubble in my eye because my contact was out of alignment. I ripped them out right in the middle of the match and started playing with glasses. I actually ended up playing a pretty good series, but having bad eyesight is always a hassle during these situations when you're trying to compete in a tournament.

Now, leading up to New Orleans, I had been playing with glasses for about a month. We got to the tournament and I played the first two days with glasses, but I started getting a migraine because the sound-canceling earphones were pushing my glasses into my nose. So the last day of the tournament I switched over to contacts. I don't want to make excuses, but that is so incredibly hard for me to do. People don't get it, but it's a weird struggle that I always have to go through.

This was a strange tournament. Usually Hardpoint was our strongest game type, but at New Orleans it was our worst. Granted, we still went 9–4 over the course of the tournament, but that was our weak link at this event. On the flip side, in game types we weren't traditionally strong at, like SnD, we went 11–1 and our only loss came in our very first match. I chalk this one up to preparation. Going in, we knew that this was our weakest game type, so we just went over it more as a team. We came up with new strategies so people couldn't read us, and obviously it worked out.

Everybody was waiting for that OpTic vs. FaZe grand final, including me, but the fact that it didn't happen didn't bother me at all. I didn't care who we played. We had one goal and that was to win the tournament. When we saw that FaZe lost, we told ourselves to just clutch up and focus on winning. We all wanted to get that revenge, but I'll admit that I also felt a bit of a relief since they were the only team that had been able to beat us on LAN recently. The team who beat FaZe was Denial and that's who we were playing in the grand final. They had beat us at Champs and ended up winning that tournament, so it was no surprise to see them get this far. They had switched out one player, but we had played against their core roster three or four times this year.

You always want to come out of the winners' bracket because it's the easier road, but on the flip side, it's tough to play a team that you just watched win a huge match. Denial was on a high. They had momentum, and sure enough they rode that into our match. We lost the first Hardpoint map, but then, like we always do, we clutched up and won the next four maps in a row to win the match and the tournament. This was probably one of my worst events in all of *AW*, but FormaL played on another level. He had something crazy like twenty-four kills. Damon was incredible.

One of the benefits of finishing strong is that we ended the season with the same roster we hope to start the next season with. That is rare, and it's the first time I ever experienced it. Usually we need to make roster changes and go out to find some of the more talented

228 // OPTIC GAMING

players early so we can be situated before the start of the year. We don't need to do that. I like to think this gives us an advantage over the other teams out there who are going through roster changes. Our team right now is so good that we can probably win matches without even calling out because we're all on the same page. That type of chemistry takes a long time to build. We're lucky in that we get along. We don't fight, and when we do, we resolve our issues quickly and without any major blowups.

What people don't understand is that there will be some new teams who will have an advantage over us. Whenever good teams get together, they almost always go through that honeymoon phase where everyone is happy and you don't see any outside factors influencing their play in the game. They do great right away. A good example of a team like this was FaZe. After a roster change, they found their groove in the middle of the season. If you look back over their record since that team got together, they won their first two tournaments and then I think they got seventh. They won the next one and then got sixth. That inconsistency usually indicates that there were problems on the team. It could be personal issues. Maybe teammates don't get along or don't like each other. That can cause some issues during the game because if two players disagree, they're gonna butt heads a lot harder than players who are good friends. Those disagreements can get pretty heated, especially if each of those players thinks they're right all the time. FaZe was a great team, but they were the perfect example of a team that could sneak up on you during that honeymoon phase. Things like that happen a lot in *Call of Duty*.

Advanced Warfare is done. I can't say enough about this past season. This was the longest season with the biggest crowds and some of the best tournament wins, but it was also the season that went the fastest. I'm sad to see *AW* go. It was a game where you couldn't be lazy. It kept me engaged and it challenged me. I don't think I'd be going out on a limb by saying that we just wrapped up OpTic Gaming's most successful year on the competitive side.

PART 7

OPTIC TODAY AND TOMORROW

30

A LONG WAY FROM OHIO

Fwiz

I never wanted to be that guy who only played video games, or who was just a commentator. Some people do and that's perfectly fine, but my ambitions were different. I gravitated more toward the business side because that was what I found most fulfilling. Now that I work at YouTube running the gaming business, my job is to create opportunities for players and creators to make a living.

I love working with people to develop products and create the actual framework for gaming to become a sustainable business. I'm a spokesman for the company, so I get to travel the world. Last year I was at the Tokyo Game Show and also made a couple of appearances on Bloomberg TV to discuss our efforts in gaming. I want to say it's a dream come true, but I never even imagined that anything like this was possible when I first fell in love with video games as a kid.

One of the most humbling moments of my career occurred in January 2015 when I learned that I made the *"Forbes* 30 under 30" for the gaming industry. This was always a list that I wanted to be on. I felt that I had a good background in gaming, but I have no idea how

I made the list or how they found me. When I learned that I was chosen, I was absolutely floored. It was crazy to see myself being grouped together with a giant like PewDiePie, who is the biggest YouTube star in the world, and also NaDeSHoT, who I have known for so long and become really good friends with. That whole experience was wild!

The one thing I still want to do one day is run my own company. Now's not the time, but one day I will. For the time being, I'm focused on continuing to make sure that people who want to be gamers and create gaming content can do it for a living. Whether you're an eSports player, an event coordinator, the guy playing *Minecraft* at home, or somebody doing parody skits, I want to continue developing this business for creators. No matter where I've worked, it's always been about helping to grow the ecosystem so it's a more viable source of income and revenue for all those involved. I did that on a creator level at Machinima, on an eSports level at MLG, and now I get to do it on a much more global scale for YouTube.

I've been so very fortunate to have a lot of things go my way—from having good friends to being able to take advantage of professional opportunities. But the one thing that I've always had trouble with is my health. It's been tough because that is completely out of my hands. What many people might not know about me is that I have Crohn's disease. I was diagnosed when I was ten. As a kid, I underwent surgery to have fourteen inches of my small intestine removed. I tried to remain positive through it all because I knew that things could always be worse. There are people dealing with substantially more difficult challenges, so if this is as bad as it can get for me, I'll take it. That's fine.

I know how tough it was for me growing up and I know there are other kids out there who are in the same situation, so I want to help them. That's why I sit on the board of a charity called Gamers Outreach. What we do is put gaming carts in hospitals. When I was in the hospital as a kid, I absolutely loved it when they would wheel in this cart with a Super Nintendo so we could play. That was one of the things that helped get me through what turned out to be a six-week stay in the hospital. I know FlamesworD from OpTic also did a charity to help raise money to put these carts in hospitals. A program like this is very close to my heart because I know what a difference it can make.

Being a leader in the industry comes with a certain responsibility to give back and look out for the players, creators, and those on the business side moving up the ranks. That's how the scene grows. I'm by no means perfect. There's a lot I need to work on personally, but I try to act like an older brother to these younger guys in the community because everyone playing *Call of Duty* now is a lot younger than me. And I'm not just talking about the OpTic boys. Players are getting younger and younger. There's a lot that happens between the ages of fourteen and twenty-two, and it's during these years when some of the most substantial life changes occur. I've always tried to set the precedent. I want to be someone those guys can look up to and I like to think that I've succeeded at that.

It's been a wild ride and I've met so many incredible people throughout the years. I love talking to people who share that same passion for gaming. I've always found it to be a cool and a very unique experience when somebody approaches me. This is especially true when it happens outside the context of a gaming event. Last year I was in New Orleans for my brother-in-law's bachelor party. We were walking down Bourbon Street when somebody stopped me: "Fwiz, can I get a picture with you?" Here I was on Bourbon Street in New Orleans. What? My friends couldn't wrap their heads around it. Even I don't know if I'll ever fully process it. Maybe one in like a hundred times when I go out in public someone will recognize me. I'm not a Hollywood star or anything, so it's kind of perfect. It's just enough where it's such a cool experience when it happens and it's never annoying.

That alone is a sign of how much eSports and *Call of Duty* have grown over the years. I think they're only going to get bigger. We finally have that developer support. What Activision is doing and the incredible hires they are making are a huge step in the right direction. This is what needs to happen to help the sport grow. It's encouraging that they've recognized the importance of having some control over the brand. It feels like they are just doubling down on how serious they are and that alone will help ensure future success. A part of me feels like things are only getting started and I can't wait to watch what happens next.

31

MY CAREER IN GAMING

OpTicJ

Growing up as a kid who was infatuated with gaming, I found that OpTic gave me the chance to do everything I wanted to do. The same way that some kids say they want to be a cop or a fireman because it just seems so cool when you're young—that's what I was like with video games. Even as a college grad who loved to play video games, I was still trying to figure out how to do it for a living.

Without OpTic, I don't know where I'd be. The work we did together gave me the raw experience of working with many forms of talent. I learned about the industry and how to be influential in the community. I definitely wouldn't have landed that job at Machinima if it wasn't for OpTic. I'm proud that I was able to play such a strong role in the company's growth. I was making creator acquisitions, working with sales, closing big deals, and being part of the first-ever major *Call of Duty* live stream. I like to think that I played a significant role in growing the gaming entertainment business on YouTube. From there I was able to land a position at Google and become a small-business entrepreneur in my own right as a creator. I haven't even mentioned all the people I've met and the great friends I've made in the process.

If I had to do it all over again, there is only one thing that I would want to do differently. I wouldn't have taken a three-year break from creating content on my channel. I would have continued to make videos while holding down my position in the corporate world of gaming. After being on a good run in 2010, I took a break in 2011. It got to the point where I was overwhelmed. I just couldn't come home after working a full-time job and try to be creative. With YouTube, you have to be driven like an entrepreneur, but being a YouTuber also requires a great deal of creativity. The execution of those ideas is very technical. You have to be constantly editing, posting, collaborating, and growing. It's like having two full-time jobs. It would have killed me at the time, so one of those had to go and it ended up being my channel. It's easy to look back on the past with rose-colored glasses, but I bet I could have found a way to make it work.

That hiatus made things a little tricky when I tried to pick my channel back up again in 2015. What's crazy was that the channel actually grew in subscribers over the years when I was absent, but they all became inactive. Likely they weren't even getting notifications, so when I relaunched, the numbers were nowhere close to what I used to get. Videos would get a few thousand views at best. I've seen growth over the past few months by being consistent and having good content. It was difficult to get back that audience that I had worked so hard to curate in the first place. It was like starting fresh.

Today, I approach my channel with five years' experience. I've seen people grow; I've seen people fail; and I've seen people completely blow up. When you look closely it's not hard to figure out what went right or wrong. There are different trends in gaming and viewership. When I started I was creating mostly *Call of Duty* content. I wasn't live-streaming. I was just making videos and editing. Lately, I primarily only live-stream. Basically every live stream I do is with the community. So if I'm live-streaming it's a "come play with me and we'll create this content together" approach. Even back when I started, my approach was always community-driven. My role now in OpTic is limited. I don't get to play with the guys that much anymore, though I do play with NaDeSHoT every two weeks or so. We create about four or five videos at a time.

Looking ahead, what I really want to do is be able to head back into an entrepreneurial-type role with all the skills and experience that I've gained. That might be through my own personal venture or a completely different business where my skills are transferable. I do know that I will be a part of managing and building a living off gaming one way or another. That might be as a personal-content creator, managing top YouTube talent, or starting companies with that talent. I will always be a part of it, but I have aspirations to be a business owner using all that gaming has taught me.

OpTic will continue to build on our reputation as the biggest and most recognizable name in eSports. I'm confident that we will grow and branch out, though it's not yet clear how. No matter how big we grow, we will never lose sight of content creation and eSports. It then becomes about how we are able to monetize what we're already good at even more effectively. How can we, with relevant partnerships, brands, and companies, utilize our resources and talent to develop those partnerships? We can't lose sight of our fans and the community, but have to be looking to double and triple down on what we're good at to ultimately impact gaming for the greater good. That might be through different charities or growing the space. OpTic should be that well-rounded company that continues to push the boundaries.

There is now much more competition. New organizations with new backings and new ideas can capitalize on those same goals that only we used to have. There is now the ability for other people to be first to a deal. That competition is what helps us to stay sharp and maintain that edge.

32

KEEP ON KEEPIN' ON

MiDNiTE

I t's hard to believe that it's been almost six years since I joined OpTic. In that time I've seen them come so far and do so many things I never thought possible. The scary part is that I can only see the organization getting bigger.

People ask me all the time what I would be doing if I wasn't gaming on YouTube and the honest answer is that I have no idea. I could be working at a factory, for all I know. I might have decided to go back to school. When I started, I was playing games for fun and partially as an escape. Whether it was school, work, family, or a relationship that was bringing me down, video games were my distraction from all that. I never thought of it as a possible job. Are you kidding? It's now become such a major part of my life that I can't picture what I'd do without it.

I'm so lucky to be able to do something I absolutely love for a living and I would be so happy to keep doing what I've been doing. Right now I have so much freedom. That's what I like and it's really hard to let that go because I know how rare of an opportunity this has been for me. I also know nothing lasts forever, and I don't know how long it'll be possible for me to keep doing this. When that day does come I'd love to be able to get a job within the *Call of Duty* community if possible. I know people that have gone on to work for developers. That would be cool, but I also like the idea of being able to work in journalism geared toward the gaming world. Who knows?

Five years ago I never would have thought I'd have close to six hundred thousand YouTube subscribers. I'm the type of person who's going to ride the wave, and if it works it works, and if it doesn't I can always go back to school for something new and try that. You have to find your passion. Right now I still have my sight set on getting one million subscribers. Even though I know the number is not all that's important, it's kind of a goal I have for myself and I think it's attainable. I have no idea how long it will take me. My channel could blow up or it might take me another five years. Who knows? I've seen people who have started after me get there.

I know I've talked about a couple less-than-fun fan experiences, but I love the relationship I have with fans and subscribers. It's way more positive than negative. For me, streaming was always the number one way to connect with fans. Over the years I began to attract regulars. I found these hard-core fans who were willing to wake up early just to catch my stream and I've actually gotten to know some of them really well. We share things on Chat. I talk with some about their relationships and doctor visits. It feels like I'm hanging out with friends and that's why I love to do it.

At the last *Call of Duty* Champs in Los Angeles, I bumped into this one fan who had been incredibly supportive of me and my channel. He was there wearing a MiDNiTE T-shirt. It is so incredibly cool when something like this happens and not creepy at all. There are some genuinely cool people out there. Every event I attend I also notice that there are more and more girls. Granted, some of the girls go there to play weird dating games and it seems like they're looking for attention or want to see their boyfriends play, but there are others who just think it's awesome. Those are the ones I always connect with.

I'm all for the growth of the girl gamer scene, but aside from the series I made when I first joined OpTic, I kind of took a step back. I never wanted to be that pick-me-up leader or spokesperson who would revolutionize the way girls are viewed in gaming. I feel that doing my own thing kind of speaks for itself.

Now there are girls out there trying to put together all-girl teams, and even co-ed teams, just to compete because they want to be on the same level. I know there is an all-women's league in *Counter-Strike*. I never really thought that all-girls' teams were the best idea. Video games aren't a physical sport, so there is no reason why guys shouldn't play with girls and vice versa. A part of me feels like that type of seg-regation only draws attention to it when the whole point is to play together and belong, but it's still pretty cool to see something like that, so I'm a little torn.

The thing that would be really cool to see is a girl playing on a top competitive team alongside guys. I don't know of any girls who have placed well at professional events. I know there are girls who have won local LAN tournaments with guys, but as far as MLG or UMG is concerned, there haven't been any girls who have competed on that level, to my knowledge. The main reason is because it's so hard to reach that level—even for a guy. It takes so many hours and finding a team that is the right fit with the right chemistry. It's hard to have a full-time job or go to school if you're playing competitive *Call of Duty*. You need not only the time, but you also need the skill. It's rare to find a guy who fits those criteria, and there are even fewer girls playing competitively, which is probably why we have yet to see it happen.

I'm sure there is that one badass chick out there who does it one day. I would love to see that happen. If she does come along, I'm sure somebody out there would give her a shot. Organizations want that player who stands out and will attract attention. It will get more eyes on the team and help them get sponsors. I think there is a desire to find girls who can do it, but the right one hasn't emerged yet.

I always thought playing competitively would be something so cool to do, but I never had the talent or the time to make pursuing this goal worthwhile. Besides, I just really like entertaining and that's what I'm going to keep doing for as long as you all make it possible.

33

LIVIN' THE DREAM

BigTymeR

The game has been good to me. You guys give me a lot of shit, but you're good to me too. I wouldn't be here without you and you've changed my life for the better. The past couple of years have been a wild ride. It's been a good time and I've made a lot of good friends, but there is one thing that I wish I could go back and change.

The biggest regret I have is the way we as a team went about releasing MerK. A lot of people were upset about that. It was a weird time in the house and we went on YouTube and made this video where it seemed like we were trying to diagnose him with clinical depression. We were throwing that word around like it wasn't something serious. I think that hurt his feelings and it obviously wasn't the right way to go about it. So if we could go back I would definitely be more professional about that and leave some of the personal stuff off YouTube because not everything needs to be broadcast to the public.

When we started playing competitive video games, there wasn't a road map. Looking back at it now, there are some things we could have done differently. If you ever watch the FaZe House videos, their whole thing is collaborating, whereas we had a competition with our-selves and that was our strategy. We wanted to make sure our stuff was all different from each other's, so we did our own thing in our own videos. At the FaZe House, they do the complete opposite. They set out to make videos with everyone in them. They help support each other and comment on each other's videos while promoting each oth-er's channels. That turned out to be a much more successful model. All of their individual channels just exploded. That seems to be the proven strategy, which was surprising to me because I wouldn't have thought it would be.

Our channels still grew tremendously, but I don't think I've ever been able to put the sheer number of people watching my ass into perspective. At any given time, I might have two thousand people watching my stream, and I'll even tell them that if there were two thousand people standing in front of me watching me do what I do, I would freak out. There's no way I could do it. Even being recognized out in public for what we do is strange. It's hard to get used to that and I'm not sure if I'll ever get used to it, but I've still had some really cool interactions with fans. One that stands out happened during *Black Ops 1* when I was able to meet the first real friend I ever made gam-ing as a kid—Blake Nored. I still talk to him today and he's probably stoked to get mentioned in the book. We basically grew up playing together online, so it was pretty cool to meet him, but I'm usually a quiet and reserved guy. I don't like too much attention, so it's weird that I've found myself becoming one of these D-list celebrities who are famous on the Internet.

That success gave me the opportunity to try out a lot of really cool things that I wouldn't otherwise have had the opportunity to do. Remember when I told you a couple chapters ago not to take time off if you're trying to build a YouTube channel? Well, that's exactly what I did in 2014. I took the whole damn year off. At the time I had about

$40,000 saved up from tournament winnings and whatnot, and I was talking with my mom about what to do with it.

Some of you probably already know this story, but I was always fascinated by the idea that money can make you more money if you know where to put it. And I knew nothing about stocks or risk management, so I learned as much as possible. The same way I got nerdy with the videos, I got nerdy with the stock market. I started to dabble, so I'd make a couple thousand and then lose a couple thousand until I learned about medicinal marijuana stocks. All I saw was how much I could earn. I dove straight in at the start of February and caught this massive, massive move. The swings in my account were like a video game. Some days I'd start off losing $30,000 and then I'd end the day up $40,000. By the end of the month I turned that nest egg into almost $1 million! I was blown away. Then the bubble burst, and I took a hit, but wound up making a good chunk of change.

Once I get interested in something, I dive in 100 percent. It was like that with *Call of Duty*. It was like that with YouTube and then it was like that with stocks. In my head, it's tough for me to stop until I'm the absolute best. More importantly, I learned this skill that I hope will last a lifetime. Even if I don't end up doing it as a job, I'll be able to take advantage of opportunities when I'm thirty-five or forty. I only spend a couple hours a day studying and trading now, but when I started I was doing it twelve hours a day. That's why I took the whole year off. There is a ridiculous amount of information that you have to process and it requires a lot of trial and error, so this has to be something you really enjoy doing. If you're only in it to make money, you'll probably flunk out in the first couple of months. Luckily, it was something that I was naturally drawn to. I enjoyed studying the market, so it came a little easier to me. I find it similar to gaming. I know a lot of old video-game players and poker players turn to stock trading. It's sort of like a video game in that the object is to get your account as high as possible while abiding by certain rules.

So, will I ever come back to playing competitive *Call of Duty*? That is a question that I get asked every single day. The problem is that I haven't really played the game in two years. I only played *Advanced Warfare*, which was a pretty good game, for like a total of twenty hours. That's not a lot. I do want to get back into the swing of things during *Black Ops 3*. I think this game will bring back those members of the *CoD* community who have recently drifted away. The way the scene is growing, it's had me thinking about maybe coming back, especially after hearing the rumors about the amount of prize money to be won. I feel like it would be a waste of my God-given talent and years of *Call of Duty* experience not to reap the real rewards that are now coming along.

Boy, I wish it were that easy. I don't doubt that I could do it, but it's a big commitment that would force me to put most everything else in my life on hold. If I sat down and just focused on playing the game, I figure it would probably take me about three months before I got back up to that level. It's mostly reaction time and raw gun skill— being able to tag enemies in the game real quick. As far as the strategy in the game modes, they're still playing Hardpoint, Capture the Flag, and Search and Destroy, which I still remember how to play. That part is not what's difficult; it's being able to make the time commitment. So . . . we'll see.

34

WHAT NOW?

NaDeSHoT

When you have the biggest following but you're not the best player, the criticism will always outweigh any positive reinforcement. The negative comments will stick out in your head more than anything supportive. You're not supposed to say this, but I think most everyone has a problem separating the two.

Nothing better exemplifies this dilemma that I've experienced throughout my career more than when I was named eSports Player of the Year in 2014. I am honored and humbled by the award, don't get me wrong, but it was a fan vote. Since I had the biggest following in eSports, I was going to win. I have a lot of loyal fans, so that was a really cool experience. Of course, all the people who said I suck came out of the woodwork. But even I knew that I wasn't the best player in eSports. I even said it in my speech. I said, "I'm sure a lot of you guys are surprised to see me up here." It was the first thing I said onstage, but looking back on it, I think it might have come off as pompous. People thought I was saying it sarcastically, but the point I was trying to make was that I knew that I wasn't the best player in eSports. I'm not the best player in *Call of Duty* or even on my own team, so how can I compare myself to these people I just beat out for this award?

The award goes to show that I do have fans who support me and without them I wouldn't be here, so I don't want to make it seem like I'm ungrateful or only harping on the negative. I do need to take time to acknowledge the positive support because it means a lot and is so incredibly important to me, so thank you guys so much for that.

As I write this today it's been about seven months since I stopped competing. I miss the excitement that comes with trying to win an event. I miss being in the booth during the finals when everything is on the line. I miss the thrill of winning right after a tournament and being on top of the world. It's that thrill of competing that I fell in love with at the very beginning. Trying to go out there and prove that being the best is not something that can be easily replicated, but the grind is tough and it requires sacrifice.

For me, as a twenty-three-year-old, I need to figure out what I'm going to do for the rest of my life. I need stability, and competitive *Call of Duty* isn't stability. Even if you win every single event of the year, which is almost impossible and something I'd never be able to do, the financial opportunity is just not there. For me, streaming and YouTube have the most stability. I would love to be able to compete again, but my main priority has to be my future. I owe that to Matthew Haag. I'm not saying that it's all about the money because it's not, but there is a practical aspect to this that a lot of people don't completely understand. That is why right now I'm leaning more toward full retirement.

I have more freedom and more opportunity now that I stopped playing competitively, but it's still very much a grind for me. I'm still making videos and streaming every single day. That is hardwired into my brain because I've been doing it for so long, but I also have the freedom to branch out and do new things. I've always toyed around with the idea of being a consultant for competitive gaming. I have years of experience in the space and can help make a game better, but I'm doing well enough on YouTube and streaming, so I don't have to worry about something like that right now.

I also want to enjoy my life. I have a girlfriend, which is phenomenal, and she gives me balance. If I'm not hanging out with her, my brain is going a mile a minute. I've always had real bad anxiety and have been dealing with that for the past ten years. Just because I stopped playing competitively doesn't mean that it went away.

Even if I don't play competitive eSports, I still want to be involved in the community. That's why I'm going to be making videos about competitive *Call of Duty* and supporting the scene. I think it's important for the community to have strong figureheads so when these companies look to invest in competitive *Call of Duty* there is someone representing them in a mature manner. I grew up with *Call of Duty* and fell in love with the game, so I still want to be a part of it. It's great to now see that the scene is stronger than ever. The direction Activision is taking is exactly what needs to be done. I wish they had done something like this two or three years ago, but better late than never. I'm happy to finally see someone taking competitive *Call of Duty* seriously.

When *Black Ops 3* comes out, I'm just going to play the game and see how I feel, but I'm leaning toward not coming back and retiring for good. Things may change. If I'm good at the game and enjoy it, we'll see what happens, but right now I just have my own personal life that I love. It feels like I have some freedom to do what I want for the first time ever.

35

ALREADY FOCUSED
ON NEXT YEAR

Scump

said it at the very beginning and I'm still saying it: I'm one of the lucky ones. Since I started playing competitively, I've had great people helping me out with the game. I'll give full credit to Rambo. He taught me how to play *Call of Duty* at a smarter level. And I've always had great teammates who I could sit down with and talk to about the game.

I'm the most competitive person in the world. Maybe not the most, but I'm up there. I don't have to look beyond my team for motivation. Right now Crimsix is the winningest player in *Call of Duty* history and has six more championships than me. He's the same way as me and we feed off each other. When we started losing to FaZe this past season, we were just so enraged. We weren't having that and practiced harder and harder.

When NaDeSHoT left the team after Champs, I feel like I stepped up to fill his leadership role. When we were down I tried to keep my team's head in the game so we didn't lose sight of the main goal. During all of those times when we went down 0–2 and we were one map away from losing the series, that's when I made sure to step up and rally the team. I know I can still get better as a player. One of my biggest issues is getting frustrated during the game when I'm not doing as well as I should be. My head gets a little cloudy during those moments, so I've tried to compensate this year by being more of a team player. I know that I don't have to dominate every map because I now have teammates who can do that for me. I just have to fill my gaps, communicate, and keep the team's morale high.

I don't see myself retiring from competitive *Call of Duty* anytime soon. I'm just trying to ride this until I don't think I can compete anymore, which won't be at least for another three or four years. I think I have a lot left in the tank. I'm still in my prime, and even when that window closes, it's not like I'm instantly going to drop off. If you still have love for the game, and that competitive drive, you can go as long as you want to go. If you look at different games like *Counter-Strike,* some of these pros are thirty years old.

There's still a lot that I need to do, like win Champs next year. *Call of Duty* Championships is the only tournament that I have yet to win. I've placed third before, but that team was not close to being as good as this recent team. I thought *AW* was going to be the year it would happen. As soon as the *AW* season ended, I already had my sights on Champs. It's not even a question of being more prepared because I think we were very well prepared at Champs this past year and had been playing a lot, but it's all about clutching up and making sure we don't choke.

After New Orleans, we had about a three-week off-season where everyone could relax before the release of *Black Ops 3*. I went and played some more *Black Ops 2* just to get the feel of it again even though it isn't on the next-gen console. I played a lot of *Destiny* and some of the other games I don't get to play as much. I wish I had the time to start a second channel and play more games. If there is a downside to competitive, it's that the players have to practice so much and play the same game so much that I don't get to enjoy that whole gaming experience. So a second channel is something I have my eye on down the road, but for right now it's all about the competitive, baby.

I don't want to go and piss people off by saying we're the "best" *Call of Duty* team ever because we still have a lot we need to do. I will say this: I think our current OpTic team is the most talented that has ever played the game. Some people would argue that CompLexity during *Black Ops 2* and *Ghosts* was better because they won more. They were fundamentally sound, but in my personal opinion, we are more talented and I hope to prove this next year. But if we dominate next year like we did this past year, I think I will be able to say that we're the best competitive team ever created.

36

BRING IT ON

H3CZ

It feels like everything that has happened was meant to be. It started with my parents leaving Mexico and moving to Chicago. Fast-forward to OpTic's venture into eSports. We lost almost every single tournament and then we won the one that mattered—the million-dollar tournament at *CoD* XP. A few years later we went on a long losing streak only to come back and win the first-ever X Games. You couldn't write a better story for OpTic.

Rosters have changed and players have come and gone, but one thing that's remained consistent has been the fan support. One of OpTic's goals from the very beginning was to cater to the people who loved *Call of Duty*. The Green Wall fans are like our little brothers, but I also think of them like our parents, in a sense. And like a proud parent, you're never going to be disappointed with your child if they're trying their best. Yeah, there's a lot of shit-talking from some fans, but the support is always there. Sometimes it's easy for the pro players to focus so much on the fifty people telling them that they suck that they forget about the hundreds of thousands cheering them on. There are far more supporters than there are haters.

The fans also get it now. They understand the decisions I make. The trust I've developed with the fans is stronger than ever. Even when my decisions may seem nonsensical, I think fans understand that they will eventually see the reasoning behind them. They know I will do what will benefit OpTic as a whole and not just one person.

The beauty of eSports is that it's always been an interactive experience. In no other form of competition at the professional level does the fan have as much of a chance to engage with the pro players. The conversations are ongoing and friendships are forged. I've never seen pro players in other sports follow their fans back on Twitter. There've been many times when a conversation that started on Twitter, or an inside joke made late one night online, carried over to an actual in-person conversation during an event. The connection between the players and fans of eSports puts everybody on an equal playing field.

The scene is only going to get bigger. The number one thing that has prevented the growth of *Call of Duty* since it began as an eSport has been the lack of developer support. David Vonderhaar was always the one, and the only one from a developer standpoint, who really pushed to make a change. Now that he's back in the driver's seat and Activision is starting to give their support to the scene, I see *Call of Duty* succeeding. Look at what we've been able to build without their help. Now that they're stepping into the space to lend a hand the way that other developers have with other games, I anticipate an explosion in *Call of Duty*. I have nothing but high hopes for this upcoming season and beyond.

Now, when anybody signs on to play the game, they will be able to read announcements for ongoing tournaments. This gives fans the option to watch the best of the best. Some kids just hop on when they're bored, but now might decide to tune in to watch instead of playing. This helps viewership and will help to attract the casual fans who are curious to learn what competitive *Call of Duty* is all about.

Who knows? It might even spark their desire to become professional players themselves and take the game a little more seriously. Maybe there is that kid out there who doesn't know much about competitive *Call of Duty*, but has been dominating every game that he was in. Now, after clicking on that link, he gets that fire to become the best when he sees the pros play. All any young competitor wants is the opportunity to play at the next level. When it comes to something like eSports, it's all about exposure. More people know what it takes to become a pro football player or pro basketball player. That doesn't make it any easier, but with eSports not everybody knows what's possible. The way we do it is by making the scene and making the players more visible. This is the same exact philosophy behind content creation.

There might be some bumps in the road during year one. With the involvement of the developer inevitably comes a little more government. There will be setbacks here and there, but that's okay. Up until now, *Call of Duty* has operated in a very small space compared to more global eSports like *League of Legends* and *Dota*. I predict that in two or three years, *Call of Duty* will be up there with the best of the best in eSports.

With more exposure comes more popularity and ultimately more competition. I welcome more competition and I want nothing more than to have other teams grow to be as big as ours because it would strengthen the entire sport. The rivalry between OpTic and FaZe was great this past year. I've always said that if we were able to create two more OpTics and two more FaZes, I think we would be considered one of the biggest eSports in the world.

I hope that rivalry continues into next season. We'll be ready and I have all the confidence in the world that OpTic can be just as successful. I can't wait to see what our competitive team does during *Black Ops 3*. The goal for next year will be to get Seth a victory at the *Call of Duty* Championships. It's the only thing that's missing from his résumé. I know he's going to go hard and that his team will go hard to get what will help solidify his position as the best player in the game. I look forward to seeing it happen. It's going to be a blast.

I want to be there every step of the way. I don't ever envision taking a step back and letting go of OpTic. Never! Even if I were to put someone in place as CEO, that CEO would have two jobs—a very fun one that involves running OpTic and a very stressful one that involves listening to me talk about next steps every single day.

Maybe it finally is time to expand into other eSports. The reason why we never expanded before was because I always felt a responsibility as the biggest team in *Call of Duty* to stay focused on this scene until it could sustain itself. Now that we're getting closer to that becoming a reality, I see us expanding into other eSports sooner rather than later. There are a lot of things in the works and we're in very good shape going into 2016.

ACKNOWLEDGMENTS

H3CZ

I would like to thank Judith, my beautiful wife, without whom none of this would be possible. Her support in the early stages of this team is what built the foundation of this amazing organization. I would also like to thank my daughter, Olivia, who is my everyday inspiration and drive; and my *jefita,* Irma, and my pops, Hector, whose sacrifice and love molded me into the man I am today. Additionally, I would like to thank my sisters, Bianca and Genesis; the Villegas family; my MVP & Villains family; and my best friend, Pedro Rodriguez, who is an amazing father and the best brother any man could ever ask for. Thank you for steering OpTic toward content creation, you literally changed my life.

NaDeSHoT

I'd like to thank my family and friends for sticking by my side through this long journey. More so, thank you to every single person that has ever supported OpTic Gaming, you have truly changed all of our lives forever.

Scump

I want to thank my mom, Kristen. Her support and encouragement in my professional career have been instrumental in my development as a player, while her unconditional love and patience have taught me how to be a good person. Thank you to my brother, Jordan, who was an amazing person to compete against growing up and was the influence for my fair and competitive nature. Finally, I want to thank my friend and father, Shawn, for his support and guidance in competition both in sports and in eSports.

BigTymeR

I'd like to thank my family and friends for being so supportive of my gaming habit, everyone involved in the creation and expansion of OpTic Gaming, and, most important, the supporters who allow us to live out our dreams each and every day. You guys are the best. #GreenWall

MiDNiTE

I would like to thank my father, Gene; my mother, Joyce; my sister, Sydney; and all of my family who have supported me throughout my life. I would also like to thank Hector and the OpTic Gaming family for the opportunities and guidance. Thank you to all of the supporters, past and future.

OpTicJ

1. Jesus, for His grace and care over my life
2. Adriana Musselman, my wife, who loves without thought
3. Hector Rodriguez, my friend, groomsman, and trusted business partner in OpTic Gaming for ten years
4. Matt Benton, my brother in Christ and colleague, who has honorably entrusted me to help grow our marketing firms: FuelRocket .net and TrenchlessMarketing.com

Fwiz

Ever since I can remember, I've loved video games. I love the way they challenged me, and the way they took me away from the day-to-day and introduced me to a whole new world. I want to thank Mama and Papa Fwiz, Melissa and Mike, for understanding this passion and properly guiding me toward making it into a career. I also want to thank my OpTic Gaming family, to whom I owe so much of my success. The individual effort each team member puts into OpTic has allowed every team member to achieve uncommon and extraordinary results in their lives. Most important, none of this happens without the #GreenWall. Ain't no fans in the damn land better than an OpTic fan!

#TheOpTicShoutOut

The OpTic Family, who has been instrumental in our growth and has had a direct impact on our success: Ian "Crimsix" Porter, Matthew "FormaL" Piper, Damon "Karma" Barlow, Marcus "MBoZe" Blanks, Michael "FlamesworD" Chaves, Michael "Di3seL" Carr, Nick "MaNiaC" Kershner, Logan "Predator" Keesling, Andrew "Ice" Peterman, Megan "Jewel," Shaun "Hutch" Hutchinson, Austin "Pamaj" Pamajewon, Alejandro "Black" Garcia, Michael "CoRoSiV3" Lorito, and Tom "Syndicate" Cassell.

Our peers/friends, who constantly challenge us to be better content creators and competitors: FaZe, nV, SIDEMEN [SDMN], Captain Sparklez, Seananners, Mr Sark, TmarTn, Jericho, Goldglove, Ali A, Hike the Gamer, Typical Gamer, and countless others who are too many to name.

Our sponsors, who have helped us along the way: Scuf Gaming, Astro Gaming, Gymshark, and Lootcrate. And a special thanks to Duncan Ironmonger and Scott Tidwell from Scuf; Aaron Drayer, Cole Lovelady, Walter Duccini, and Enrique Espinoza from Astro;

Dan Crane from Gymshark; and Matt Arevalo, Matt Eitel, and Chris Darbro from Lootcrate.

Thank you to Dan Ciccone and our partners at rEvolution and rEvXP, for leading the way in eSports marketing for brands, and Dario Raciti and our friends at OMD, for believing in the power of OpTic Gaming and eSports.

Thank you to the leagues MLG, Gfinity, and UMG, who have kept *Call of Duty* eSports alive; and last but certainly not least, thanks to Activision Publishing, for creating *Call of Duty*, the game that brought us all together, as well as to all the studios that made it happen, Infinity Ward, Treyarch, Sledgehammer—with special thanks to David Vonderhaar, Robert Taylor, and Jay Puryear, for their hard work in *Call of Duty* eSports.

Thank you to Matt Harper from HarperCollins for giving OpTic a platform to tell our eSports story.

Thank you to Enrique Espinoza.

Thank you to Bill Kenney for his help on this project.